GIMP for Absolute Beginners

■ ■ ■

Jan Smith
with Roman Joost

Apress®

GIMP for Absolute Beginners

ISBN-13 (pbk): 978-1-4302-3168-4

ISBN-13 (electronic): 978-1-4302-3169-1

President and Publisher: Paul Manning
Lead Editor: Dominic Shakeshaft
Technical Reviewer: Alexandre Prokoudine
Editorial Board: Steve Anglin, Mark Beckner, Ewan Buckingham, Gary Cornell, Jonathan Gennick, Jonathan Hassell, Michelle Lowman, Matthew Moodie, Jeff Olson, Jeffrey Pepper, Frank Pohlmann, Douglas Pundick, Ben Renow-Clarke, Dominic Shakeshaft, Matt Wade, Tom Welsh
Coordinating Editor: Jessica Belanger
Copy Editor: Mary Behr and Kimberly Burton
Indexer: SPi Global
Production Support: Patrick Cunningham
Cover Designer: Anna Ishchenko

Distributed to the book trade worldwide by Springer Science+Business Media, LLC., 233 Spring Street, 6th Floor, New York, NY 10013. Phone 1-800-SPRINGER, fax (201) 348-4505, e-mail orders-ny@springer-sbm.com, or visit www.springeronline.com.

For information on translations, please e-mail rights@apress.com, or visit www.apress.com.

Apress and friends of ED books may be purchased in bulk for academic, corporate, or promotional use. eBook versions and licenses are also available for most titles. For more information, reference our Special Bulk Sales–eBook Licensing web page at www.apress.com/bulk-sales.

Contents

Contents

About the Author

Jan Smith has been taking photos for more than 20 years; her photos have been reproduced in a range of media. In 2000 she studied digital imaging at the Adelaide Central School of Art and moved from the darkroom to digital editing with relief.

Jan discovered GIMP nine years ago while volunteering at Computerbank (a non profit company refurbishing donated computers for low income people). She helped people become familiar with computers loaded with open-source software. She has developed a solid grasp of the way beginners learn to use software.

Jan has worked as a technical writer for Infrae in the Netherlands and for companies using open-source software in Australia. She was elected Vice President of the Zope Foundation in 2010. She has a background in radio journalism, technology and production.

Roman Joost first learned about open-source software in 1997. He is the project manager of GIMP's user documentation and he has contributed code to GIMP. He has contributed to GIMP and Zope open-source projects for eight years.

Roman has a Diplom-Informatiker (FH) from Anhalt University of Applied Sciences in Koethen, Germany. He has worked for Gocept GmbH & Co. in Germany, Infrae in the Netherlands, and is currently working for another Zope company in Brisbane, Australia. For relaxation, he enjoys photography and digital painting with GIMP.

About the Technical Reviewer

Alexandre Prokoudine is a regular contributor to various, free software projects—mostly related to design, photography, and music and video production. When not using, testing, or translating apps, he writes news about and tutorials on them for the Libre Graphics World blog. He works in the education projects department for a Linux vendor.

Acknowledgments

Thanks to my husband, Darce Cassidy, for his feedback, patience, cooking and the photo on page 73. Thanks to my son, Michael Cassidy, for his sage-like comments. Thanks to Anna Rigg for the photo on page 60. Thanks to Robyn Harvey for your friendship and encouragement. To Arthur Dent, thanks for nagging me in 1999 to get involved in open-source software, where intelligence and cooperation help overcome short-sighted, greedy, vendor lock-in.

A special thanks to Alexandre Prokoudine; the book is richer for your helpful and incisive technical review. Thanks to Roman for writing the painting and drawing chapters and for sticking with the project, even after the arrival of your first child. Thanks to Jessica Belanger, Matt Wade, Nancy Wright, Kimberly Burton, Mary Behr, Dylan Wooters, Leah Weissburg, and the team at Apress who helped whip this book into shape. Thanks also to the members of the Parklands Photo Club and others who filled out the digital editing survey.

Thanks to Jernej Simončičfor making GIMP available to Windows users and to everyone involved in the development of this powerful software.

—Jan Smith

Thanks to my family for the support they gave me; without I would have not been able to participate in this book. Thanks to Anne Schneider, my brother Lars, my wife and Ross Copping for checking my chapters and trying various exercises. Additional thanks goes to my brother Lars for his artwork in Figure 8-26 on page 198. To my uncle Dr. Wolfgang Joost, a dedicated thanks for your inspiration.

I would like to thank Jan Smith for the countless effort she put into this book and her support in general. Without her, this book would have not been possible.

Thanks again to the many GIMP developers and people in the free software community, like Sven Neumann, Michael Natterer, Alexandre Prokoudine, Martin Nordholds, and many more who helped me contribute to this application. Thanks to the documentation team who put in a lot of effort into making the GIMP user manual better with each release.

I would also like to thank Jakub Steiner and Garrett LeSage for their contributions to the free software community; they inspired me to contribute, too.

—Roman Joost

Introduction

Is This Book for You?

- Yes, if you are moving from a photographic darkroom to a digital image editor.

- Yes, if you are looking for a digital image editing guide for beginners.

- Yes, if you enjoy using free software.

- No, this book is not for you if you want to use the command line or scripting (see GIMP's online resources for assistance).

What Is GIMP?

GIMP is a digital image editor and a digital drawing tool. GIMP allows you to:

- Retouch photos by fixing problems affecting the whole image or parts of the image

- Adjust colors in your photos to bring back the natural look

- Be creative with your photos—crop, blend, and add items, special effects, and more

- Discover the fun of digital drawing and painting without messy paints and a wet canvas

If you need something more than a simple digital editing program, GIMP could be for you. GIMP has the ability to sandwich different elements to make up a picture. It also has controls for cropping, scaling, exposure, brightness, contrast, color balance, sharpening, and a vast number of ways of selecting objects in an image. There are a large number filter effects for photos and drawings. Images can convert to a large range of file formats.

Volunteer programmers, designers, and writers have been developing GIMP for more than fifteen years. The 2012 release of GIMP version 2.8 has new features, such as Single-Window Mode and Paint Dynamics. GIMP traditionally has three separate windows. Single-Window Mode joins the three windows into one workspace. With Paint Dynamics enabled, brush strokes mimic real-world brush strokes.

GIMP for Windows, Mac, and Linux

This book covers GIMP 2.8 and explains GIMP for Windows, Mac, and Linux. If you have an older version of GIMP, please upgrade so that you can use GIMP's latest features, which are described in this book. GIMP is free to upgrade because it is free software.

Why Does GIMP Have an Odd-Sounding Name?

This is a question often asked of the GIMP community.

GIMP stands for **GNU Image Manipulation Program.** It was originally called The GIMP, but today the correct name is GIMP. Developers of GIMP are happy with this name.

This Book Is for Beginners

This is book is written for absolute beginners to digital image editing and digital drawing. We presume you have a working knowledge of your computer, its operating system, how to use a mouse, and find items in a menu system. You should also be able to find your images on your computer. We do not expect you to have used GIMP or any other digital image editing software. This guide is to help you get up and running editing your images using a wide range of options and to get started with digital drawing.

Some people have the luxury of learning digital image editing in a classroom with the help and support of teachers and other students. This book presumes you have no one to turn to for help or for encouragement with your GIMP project.

There is nothing like the exhilarating feeling of transforming an ordinary image into a very good or even a great image. It is not so great if you are stuck or if you do not know how to do something in GIMP. It is even worse if you do not know the technical name for the task that you are trying to complete. Forgetting or not knowing the technical name for a task can happen with any image-editing program, not just GIMP.

We have reduced the emphasis on technical terms such as, masks, paths, channels, layers, filters, and so on. However, this does not mean we do not cover these topics. If you know what these concepts mean, you can look them up in the index at the back of the book. Beginners using this book will get to use some or all of these concepts depending on the projects they choose to do.

The Focus Is on Problem Solving

The focus of this book is on tasks and problem solving. We tested chapters in this book with people who had never used GIMP and with people new to digital editing. We also surveyed camera club users and took note of their responses. For some, the hardest part was finding things in GIMP. Throughout the book, we help you locate tools and menu options. Some people want to jump in and start editing straight away. Others need an overview and a clear roadmap. Not everyone learns a new skill the same way. This book covers a few approaches to learning.

You can read each chapter in turn or you can just read the section that solves your current digital editing task or problem. It is your choice.

Throughout the book, we point out traps for new digital editors.

Will I Be Successful in Using GIMP?

If you use GIMP once a year, you are not going to be successful in using GIMP. To get the maximum benefit from GIMP, like anything worthwhile, you must practice. If you do not have lots of time, we suggest you learn one or two useful tasks in GIMP. It is then easy to build on this and increase your skills.

Is GIMP Too Complicated?

If you are worried that GIMP may be too difficult or geeky for you, you are probably wrong. If you can you pass exams, drive a car, cook, sew, hold down a job, or find your way around a new city with a map, then you have sufficient skills to try GIMP. If you have a fear of computers, then think of your computer as a mere tool for your creativity, rather than a barrier.

Have you used another image-editing program? Do not expect GIMP to do things exactly the same way. GIMP does some tasks differently; for instance to save a JPG image, you export it rather than save it. There may be a learning curve for you. This book tries to resolve those hiccups and differences.

Photoshop and GIMP Comparisons

You may have been using Photoshop and have decided to try GIMP. Things will not necessarily be in the same place in both programs. Our hints and tips section in Chapter 10 looks at the similarities and differences between Photoshop and GIMP. GIMP is more complex than Photoshop Elements.

Why Is GIMP Free?

People participate in open-source software for similar reasons that people play or follow a sport. They like the code and they enjoy the social aspects. Open-source developers believe in sharing knowledge freely. Working on an open-source project is a way for people to have fun, to build something they need, to share, to compete, to extend their knowledge, to help others, to be part of a community, and for some, to become well-known in that community.

The History of GIMP

The story of GIMP's development helps explain how open-source programs evolve and extend.

In 1995, two university students, Peter Mattis and Spencer Kimball, developed the first version of GIMP for a project at the University of California at Berkeley. After the completion of the class project, they decided to extend their small project. Peter worked on the plug-in architecture and Spencer worked on core GIMP. This meant they were working on very separate pieces of the architecture. They were complimentary teammates.

Collaboration and Sharing in the Open-Source World

Peter and Spencer did not develop in isolation; they participated in newsgroups and mailing lists. In July 1995, Peter answered a mailing list question about plug-ins, gave his own solution, and offered further information, if needed. A few months later, Peter asked a newsgroup, "What kind of features should (image manipulation software) have? (Tools, selections, filters, etc.) What file formats should it support?"

They were developing, sharing, evolving, and collaborating with others from the beginning.

By July 1996, GIMP had two mailing lists, the gimp-user and the gimp-developer mailing lists. In 1997, Peter and Spencer graduated from the university and stopped contributing to the GIMP project. By then, however, other people were contributing to GIMP and are continuing to do so today.

GPLv3 License for GIMP

GIMP 2.8 has a GPLv3 license. The GPLv3 license allows people to use GIMP for no charge. Additionally, developers can use or make a copy of the source code and add to it or turn it into something else entirely. Developers can distribute this new version, as long as the original code and the new code have the same sharing conditions. You can read the full license details in Appendix B.

GIMP 2.8

Released in 2012, this version of GIMP has a number of new features.

- Single-Window Mode gives the option of joining GIMP's three windows into one window.

- Single-Window Mode incorporates the navigation of open images via thumbnails.

- With Brush Dynamics enabled, the thickness and opacity of a brush depends on the pressure, speed, and angle of your mouse or graphical tablet.

- Brushes now have the option of rotation.

- There is an improved text tool.

- Enhanced resource management allows for tagging of frequently-used tools.

- Layers have a locking feature to avoid accidental strokes.

- There is improved ability to customize GIMP's tools and workspace.

- The Cage Transform Tool enables you to alter the shape of a subject, while keeping it realistic-looking.

400,000 Downloads a Week?

According to SourceForge, every week more than 400,000 people download GIMP for Windows and Mac from its web site alone.

Summary

GIMP is a sophisticated, open-source image-editing program. If you have basic computer skills, it is possible to learn GIMP. This book guides the person new to graphics and digital editing software. Use this book to solve some simple graphics tasks, then come back to the book to try tasks that are more complex.

■ ■ ■

CHAPTER 1

Finding and Installing GIMP

In This Chapter

- Where to find GIMP

- How to install GIMP on your computer

Is This Chapter for You?

- If you have installed a program on your computer before, try this chapter.

- If you have not installed a program on your computer before, ask the person who usually adds extras to your computer for help. Do not forget to hand them your usual bribe and this chapter. They will be pleasantly surprised to see how easy it is to install GIMP.

- If you want to install GIMP from the source code, this chapter is not for you. Try the online resources at www.gimp.org.

You may still be hesitating and asking yourself if you should try GIMP. GIMP is one of the very few free programs that provides an alternative to expensive advanced photo editing software such as Photoshop. If you use Photoshop and are trying GIMP for the first time, Chapter 10 covers the similarities and differences between GIMP and Photoshop. When you download GIMP, you will not be alone; there have been over 112 million downloads of GIMP for Windows.

You probably have some photos you would like to improve or play around with but you aren't sure if this will be easily accomplished. We try to make editing in GIMP as easy as possible for a beginner so you can focus on your creativity.

Will GIMP work on your computer? GIMP is available for computers with Windows, Mac, or Linux operating systems, and it needs 1GB or more of RAM. Do not put GIMP on an old computer from your garage and then blame GIMP if it runs slowly.

This chapter shows you where to find and download GIMP and how to install it for Windows, Mac, and Linux. GIMP 2.8 was used for this book, but older versions are available. However, since GIMP is free, we see no need to use an older version. And GIMP 2.8 has some very useful new features!

As mentioned, you will not be the first person to download and try GIMP.

- There are over 400,000 weekly downloads of GIMP for Windows from SourceForge.

- There are around 40,000 weekly downloads of GIMP for Mac from SourceForge.

- For Linux, it is guestimated that there are more weekly downloads than GIMP for Mac.

GIMP Works on Windows, Mac, and GNU/Linux

GIMP is available for the following Microsoft Windows systems:

- Win7

- Vista

- XP

- Windows Portable is a GIMP application for a USB drive, CD, DVD, etc.

■ **Note** Older versions of Windows can run older versions of GIMP. However, very old versions of GIMP look and behave differently than the examples given in this book.

GIMP is available for the following Apple Macintosh systems:

- Snow Leopard 10.6x

- Leopard 10.5x

- Tiger 10.4x

GIMP works on both PC- and Intel-based Macs. The GIMP for Mac download comes bundled with a number of extra photo editing and retouching tools.

■ **Note** A very old version of GIMP will run on Panther 10.3 but it lacks many of the features talked about in this book. GIMP will not run on version 9 of the Macintosh operating system.

GIMP is easy to install on the following Linux systems:

- Debian

- Fedora

- Gentoo Portage

- Slackware

- OpenSUSE

- Ubuntu

Most other versions of Linux also support GIMP but the installation may be more complicated.

System Requirements

GIMP 2.8+ runs well on computers that are one to three years old. GIMP needs 1GB of RAM to run. More RAM is definitely an advantage, especially when working on large images.

GIMP will run on Windows or Mac computer without conflicting with other graphic software such as Photoshop.

GIMP Is Free Open Source Software

GIMP is free of charge. It is not only free of charge but you are free to use and share this program with as many people as you wish. Beginners can use GIMP; in fact, this book aims to help beginners become proficient at using GIMP. At the other end of the spectrum, if you're a programmer, you're free to change the source code to suit your needs, provided you agree to keep the GIMP source code open. This means it is possible to use, share, and enhance GIMP. There is a copy of the full GIMP GNU General Public License v 3 in Appendix B.

GIMP has a large online community of users. You are welcome to be a part of this online community no matter where you live—you just need an Internet connection. GIMP is available in a large number of languages.

This chapter focuses on downloading GIMP 2.8+ released in 2012. If you have an older version of GIMP, now is the time to upgrade—GIMP is free. See the following sections for instructions for downloading and installing GIMP on Windows, Mac, and Linux.

Windows: Downloading and Installing GIMP

Downloading and installing GIMP on Win7, Windows Vista, or Windows XP is easy. Anyone who has downloaded a program on a Windows computer can do this. If you have never downloaded anything before, try now.

Close any other programs that are currently running on your computer. This is to ensure a clean installation.

To get the latest version of GIMP, you will be clicking through a few screens.

■ **Note** www.gimp.org automatically checks your computer's operating system and loads the front page with links to installing GIMP for your operating system.

---

1. Go to www.gimp.org (Figure 1-1).

Figure 1-1. *The GIMP web site*

2. Click the Download button. This takes you to the GIMP for Windows downloads page (Figure 1-2).

Figure 1-2. *GIMP for Windows download page at www.gimp.org/downloads/*

3. Click the "Download GIMP 2.8 – Installer for Windows XP sp2 or later" link. When you click the link, you will be taken to the SourceForge download center (Figure 1-3). The installer for Windows XP sp2 or later includes GIMP.

Figure 1-3. *The SourceForge download page for GIMP.*

4. If the download does not start automatically, click the Save button at the bottom of the SourceForge page. When GIMP has downloaded to your computer, a small window will pop up asking if you want to run this file. You're nearly there—just a few more clicks!

5. Click Run (Figure 1-4). If you do not see the pop-up screen, look in your Downloads folder or the folder where you normally download items from the Internet.

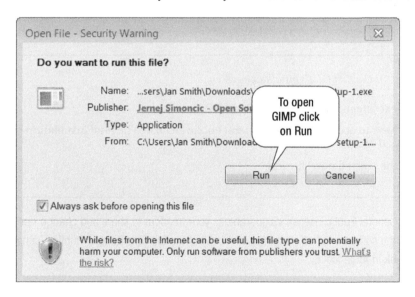

Figure 1-4. *This window pops up after GIMP has downloaded to your computer*

6. Follow the instructions in the installation setup wizard (Figure 1-5).

Figure 1-5. *The first GIMP installation screen*

The next screen has the GNU General Public License.

7. Click Next to accept the GNU General Public License. The final installation screen follows (Figure 1-6).

8. Click the "Install now" button.

■ **Note** The GNU General Public License v3 guarantees your freedom to share and change free software and to make sure the software is free for all users. A copy of the full GNU General Public License v 3 is at the back of the book in Appendix B.

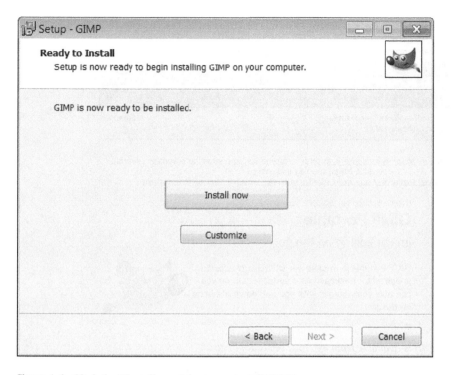

Figure 1-6. *Click the "Install now" button to install GIMP onto your computer*

When GIMP is installed on your computer, you will see a screen with the option to launch (or start) GIMP. Congratulations! GIMP is now installed.

■ **Note** The first time GIMP opens on your computer, it will take some time. GIMP is loading a number of presets and tools. Be patient. GIMP will open a lot faster after this first time.

Portable GIMP for Windows: Installing GIMP on a USB Drive, CD, or DVD

This is an optional extra for people with Microsoft Windows on their computer. GIMP is small enough to run on a USB drive. GIMP portable will run on a thumb drive/USB stick, CD, or DVD. GIMP Portable will not run as fast as if it was installed on your computer but can be very handy to have on hand.

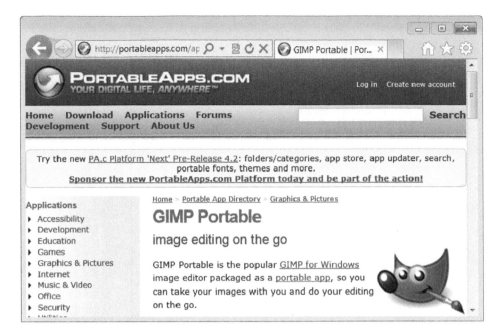

Figure 1-7. *Portable GIMP is available from www.portableapps.com*

1. Go to www.portableapps.com (see Figure 1-7).

2. Click on Applications in the top menu bar.

3. Scroll down and click on GIMP portable. You will then see the GIMP portable download area.

4. Click on the Download button.

When GIMP Portable has downloaded to your computer, it is a good idea to test the download on your desktop. Click and start GIMP Portable on your desktop. If GIMP Portable opens and runs well, your test is complete. Close GIMP Portable by clicking on File ➤ Exit. Copy the file to your USB drive, CD, or DVD.

If there is a problem with the download, delete that copy and download GIMP Portable again. This should sort out most problems.

Mac: Downloading and Installing GIMP

If you are not sure which Mac OS X operating system you have, click on the Apple logo on your top Mac menu bar and then click "About This Mac".

Check below to see if GIMP 2.8 is available for your version of the Mac operating system. Usually it's just a matter of time before GIMP is available for the latest Mac operating system.

Snow Leopard and Leopard (Mac OS X 10.6x, Mac 10.5x)

Before downloading GIMP, it is a good idea to install the latest updates of Snow Leopard or Leopard on your Mac. These general operating system updates increase the stability, compatibility, and security of your Mac. The updates are free, so go to www.apple.com/support/ and search for Snow Leopard or Leopard updates.

Now you are ready to download GIMP. To ensure you get the latest version of GIMP, you will be clicking through some web pages to get to the download area.

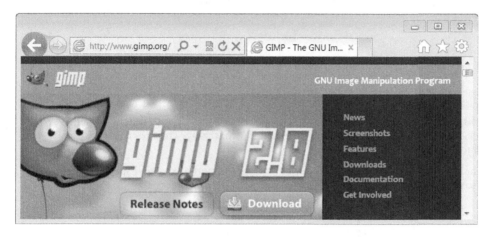

Figure 1-8. *www.gimp.org is the official Internet home for GIMP*

1. Go to www.gimp.org and click on the Download button (Figure 1-8).

2. On the next screen under the GIMP for MAC OS X heading, click the Download link (yes, a second Download click). This takes you to the web site dedicated to GIMP for Mac (Figure 1-9).

Figure 1-9. *GIMP on OS X home*

3. Scroll down and click on the correct link for your operating system. Choose one of the following: GIMP for Snow Leopard, GIMP for Leopard, or GIMP for Tiger. (You should be at the SourceForge download area, as shown in Figure 1-10.)

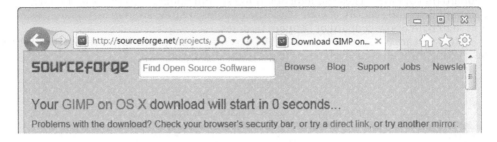

Figure 1-10. *SourceForge.net GIMP on OS X download area*

4. You may see a pop-up screen asking if you're sure you want to download GIMP. Say yes. Alternatively, the download will start automatically. The files downloaded to your Mac will end in .dmg.

5. Click on the GIMP.dmg file on your computer to open it. You will see the contents shown in Figure 1-11.

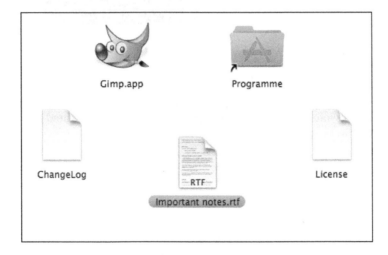

Figure 1-11. *The contents of the opened .dmg file. This file may have the word Programme instead of Application*

6. You have a choice. You can drag the gimp.app icon into the Programme folder (see Figure 1-12). Alternatively, you can drag gimp.app into your Applications folder. Either choice installs GIMP into your Applications folder.

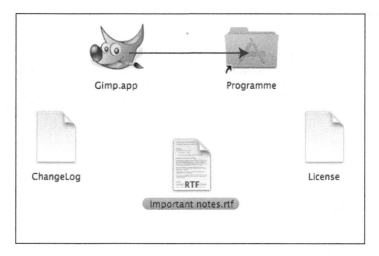

Figure 1-12. *Drag GIMP.app onto the blue Programme folder to install GIMP*

Congratulations! You can now open GIMP the same way you open any other program.

Tiger: Downloading and Installing GIMP

The GIMP Tiger installation requires an extra step: you need to install X11. You can get X11 from your Tiger installation DVD or go to the Apple Tiger support web page and follow the instructions for installing X11. After you install X11, follow the steps for Snow Leopard, discussed in the previous section. (Snow Leopard and Leopard come with X11 installed.)

■ **Note** If you have OS X 10.3 Panther, you can only run an older version of GIMP: GIMP 2.2. It will look and act differently than the examples in this book.

GNU/Linux

GIMP is available for most Linux operating systems. Look for GIMP in your Linux Applications menu. The following systems will have GIMP installed or will have an easy software installer:

- Debian
- Fedora

- Gentoo Portage
- Slackware
- OpenSuse
- Ubuntu

If these options don't work for your version of Linux, install GIMP using the package management system for your Linux distribution. The distribution maintainers check for any dependent files and do the bug fix updates for GIMP. You can also get GIMP via the command line. Both these options are beyond the scope of this beginner's book. For further information on downloading using the package management system or downloading via the command line, go to www.gimp.org.

Ubuntu

If you are new to Linux, here's how to install GIMP on one of its most popular distributions: Ubuntu. Ubuntu Lucid and later distributions don't come with GIMP installed.

Figure 1-13. *Ubuntu Applications menu showing the Ubuntu Software Centre*

1. In the top Ubuntu Menu, click on Applications and scroll down and click on Ubuntu Software Centre (Figure 1-13).

2. Type GIMP into the search box located at the top right hand corner of the Ubuntu Software Applications Centre screen (Figure 1-14).

Figure 1-14. *Type GIMP into the search box in the top right hand corner*

3. You will be taken to a list of programs. Scroll down to GIMP and click on Install.

4. When asked, type in your usual Ubuntu password.

5. You may be asked to approve extra files or dependencies for GIMP. There may also be security update files. Agree to install these files.

6. Click Install. GIMP will download and install into your Ubuntu system.

When the files are installed on your computer, GIMP will be available in the Applications/Graphics menu. The first time GIMP starts, it starts slowly because it is loading a number of tools. GIMP will start much faster next time.

Extra Functionality in GIMP via Plugins

GIMP has many plugins available to do extra things in GIMP such as editing RAW images or adding animation functionality. It's not necessary to add extra plugins. Sometimes a plugin can solve a particular task you wish to do in GIMP. This is a beginner's book so we will first focus on getting to know GIMP as it comes out of the box. Chapter 10 covers how to find and install plugins.

Summary

In this chapter you learned how to find and download GIMP 2.8+ for Windows, Mac, and Linux. Congratulations if you now have GIMP installed! With GIMP on your computer, you're ready to have some fun with digital editing. If you wish to add extra plugins to GIMP, see Chapter 10. If you know how to use Photoshop, Chapter 10 also has some tips and hints about the similarities and differences between Photoshop and GIMP.

■ ■ ■

CHAPTER 2

Getting to Know the GIMP Workspace

In This Chapter

- The quickest way to learn GIMP
- Starting GIMP
- GIMP 2.8 workspace
- Simplifying GIMP's workspace
- GIMP workspace tour
- Opening an image
- Toolbox tour
- Menus tour
- Utility docking window tour

Is This Chapter for You?

- Yes, if you are new to GIMP.
- Yes, if you have used another image-editing program and are trying out GIMP. If you know Photoshop, also look at the Chapter 10 in the "Hints and Tips" section for Photoshop comparisons.

By now you should have GIMP installed on your computer. Congratulations! One of the hardest things for most beginners is getting started. The next step, starting to use a new program, can be equally daunting. These are the two biggest hurdles for most beginners. For most people, once you have completed a couple of tasks in GIMP you will begin to relax and get used to the new processes.

In this chapter, we show you how to open GIMP and give you a tour of GIMP's tools and features. We also show you how to set the workspace to single-window mode, which makes finding things easier. The chapter has some quizzes to help you check your progress. Because this is a book for beginners, at any one time, you will be using only a couple of options. Importantly we will show you clearly where and how to do a task at the time we are discussing the task. We don't expect you to memorize this chapter. This chapter is just to give you a feel for GIMP's layout and its possibilities; you should feel free to come back here at any time.

Quickest Way to Learn GIMP

A tip to help you remember where things are in GIMP is to have a problem you want to solve, such as how to open and save an image. By the end of this chapter, you should know how to open GIMP, how to open an image, and how to see the information GIMP is giving you about your image. You should know how to find the toolbox, where the menus are located, and the options the menus provide. Finally, you will know where the dialogs or panels are located and have an overview of how they can help you.

Reading or working through this section is the fastest way to use GIMP efficiently—for some people. Not everyone learns an activity in the same way. Some people learn by doing, others need to get an overview first. If you want to start doing something in GIMP, rather than taking this tour of the interface, skip this chapter. You can always come back later.

Starting GIMP

GIMP starts the same way as other programs on your computer. If you are not sure, follow the directions below for Windows, Apple Mac, or Linux.

Windows

To start GIMP in Windows, in the bottom left hand corner of your screen, choose Start ➤ All Programs ➤ GIMP. The first time GIMP opens, it will open slowly. GIMP is configuring one-off options and directories. Don't worry; it will open faster next time.

Mac

To start GIMP in Mac, go to the Applications folder, scroll down and click on GIMP. GIMP will open slowly the first time because it is configuring behind the scenes options and directories. It will open faster next time.

Linux

GIMP starts the same way as other applications for your distribution. The latest versions of Ubuntu do not have GIMP installed. See Chapter1 for installation instructions for Ubuntu. To open GIMP, click on Applications, scroll down to Graphics; in the Graphics submenu, click on GIMP to open it. See Chapter 1 for full installations details.

What Version of GIMP Do You Have?

This book covers GIMP version 2.8. If you don't know what version of GIMP you have, click on the Help menu located at the top of the Image Window (the window with the menus on top), scroll down and click About. A small window will open with details about the version of GIMP running on your computer. If you have a version older than 2.8, consider updating to 2.8; it's free and worth the effort. Earlier versions of GIMP look a little different and don't have some of the newest features. Using an older version of GIMP will make this book more difficult to follow. See Chapter 1 to find out how to get the latest version of GIMP.

GIMP 2.8 Workspace

GIMP may look strange to you when it opens. Most new programs do seem odd at first. The relatively simple-looking windows contain a huge number of useful features and can be confusing at first glance. Don't worry, we will work through it and you'll learn where to find everything.

When GIMP 2.8 opens, you should see three separate windows, as shown in Figure 2-1.

- The Toolbox window has tools for your projects.

- The Image window is used for editing images and accessing menus.

- The Utility Docking window is available to organize layers, history, color pallets, etc.

Toolbox Window   Image Window   Utility Docking Window

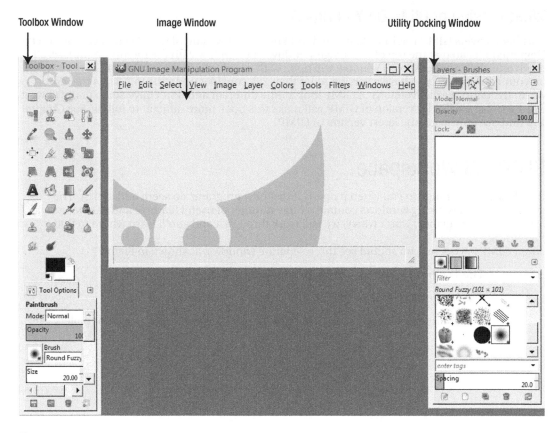

Figure 2-1. *GIMP's three windows: the Toolbox Window, the Image Window, and the Utility Docking Window*

Simplifying GIMP's Workspace

You may have opened GIMP 2.8 and not been able to see the three windows in Figure 2-1. Don't worry; there is a simple option available to fix this and it's called single-window mode.

Single-Window Mode

We suggest all beginners and people new to GIMP set up single-window mode. Single-window mode joins GIMP's three windows together. This means you will always see a combined workspace. This will save you the bother of looking for buried windows, a problem that can occur using the three-window workspace default. Figure 2-1 shows GIMP's three separate windows. Compare this with Figure 2-2, which shows GIMP in single-window mode. In single-window mode, the Toolbox window, the Image window, and the Utility Docks windows are combined into one larger window.

Flexible Workspace

The walls of the windows in single-window mode are flexible. You can drag on the internal divisions to make a window larger or smaller. You can drag on the edges to make the window taller or wider. As you start to edit you will find how useful it can be to be able to push the workspace around to suit you.

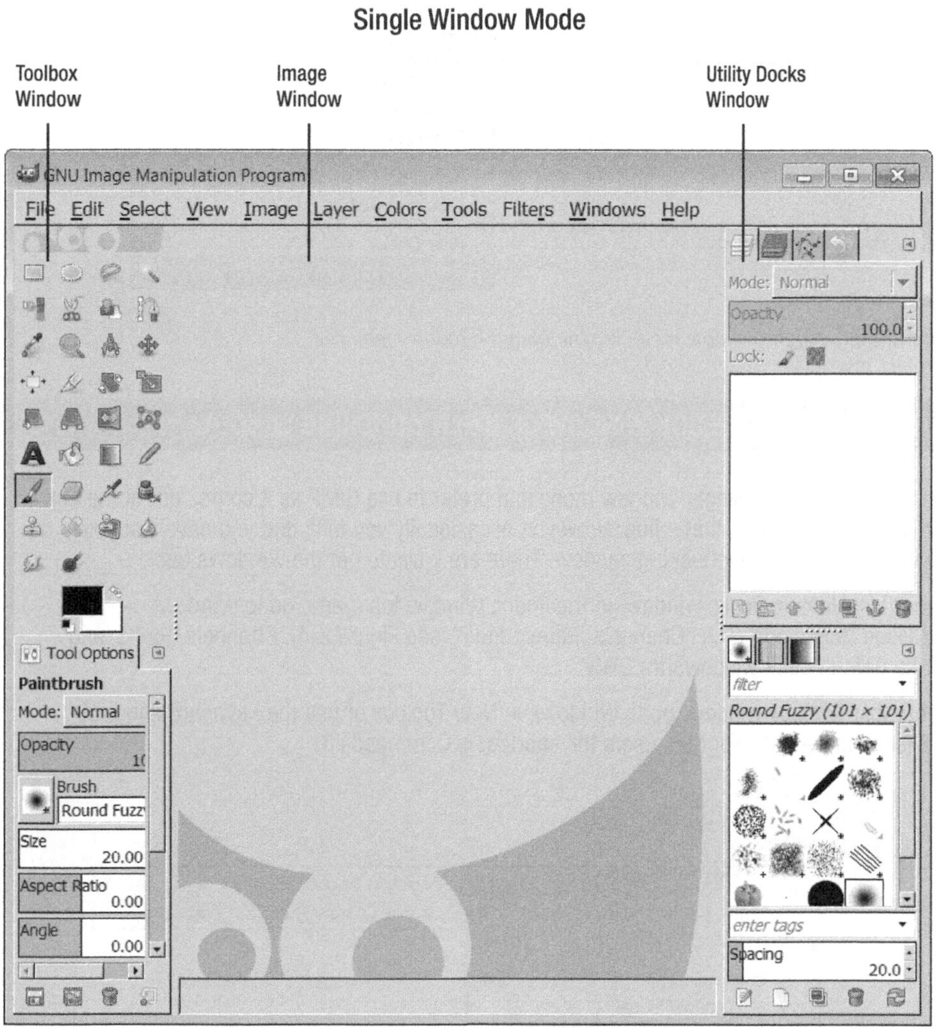

Single Window Mode

Toolbox
Window

Image
Window

Utility Docks
Window

Figure 2-2. *The Toolbox window, Image window, and Utility Docking window are joined in single-window mode. Drag on the edges and the internal divisions to see the flexibility of single-window mode.*

Getting Single-Window Mode

To change from three separate windows to single-window mode, in the Image window top menu, click Windows (see Figure 2-3). A submenu or list of options will open; scroll down with your mouse and click "Single-Window Mode."

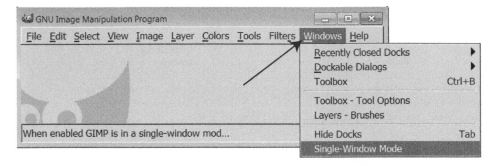

Figure 2-3. *Changing to single-window mode via the Image Window menu*

MISSING TOOLBOX WINDOW OR UTILITY DOCKING WINDOW

If you don't want to use the single-window mode and prefer to use GIMP as it comes out of the box with three separate windows, that's fine. However, occasionally you may find you have lost your Toolbox window or your Utility Docking window. There are ways to get the windows back.

To view your lost Utilities Docks window, in the Image Window top menu, go to Windows ➤ Recently Closed Docks and click "Channels, Paths, Undo" (see Figure 2-4). Channels, Paths, and Undo are the default dock windows for GIMP.

To view your lost Toolbox window, go to Windows ➤ New Toolbox or use the keyboard shortcut Control+B (see Figure 2-4). For Mac users the shortcut is Command+B.

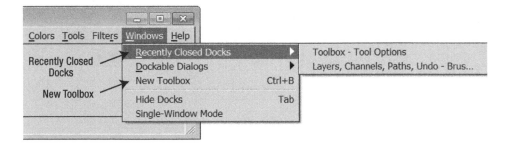

Figure 2-4. *Locating the workspace windows in the Image Window menu*

You should now see the Toolbox window, the Image window, and the Utility Docking window.

Single-Window Mode Screenshots

The screenshots in this book use the single-window mode because we believe it is the most useful mode for new users. In single-window mode, GIMP's three windows are joined together and stay together; this was a much requested feature. If you have decided to stay with the GIMP default of three separate windows, it should be easy enough to follow the instructions with the single-window mode screenshots.

Quick Quiz

With GIMP's workspace visible on your computer screen, answer the following questions.

1. Can you locate GIMP's Toolbox area?

2. Can you locate the image editing area?

3. Can you locate the utility docking area?

Don't worry if you have no idea what these areas do. You need to know where things are before you can perform any actions.

GIMP Workspace Tour

Before you can do most things in GIMP, it's essential to know how to create, access, and open a image. A blank image is useful for painting and drawing. As a beginner, it's also useful to have a blank image open when you explore the tools in the Toolbox.

Opening a Blank Image

1. In the top menu, click File (see Figure 2-5).

2. In the drop-down File menu, click New.

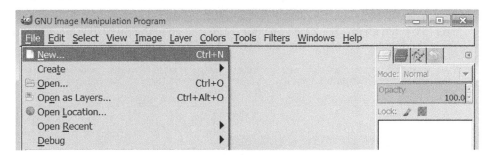

Figure 2-5. *To open a blank image, go to File ➤ New.*

3. A small dialog called the Create a New Image window pops up (see Figure 2-6).

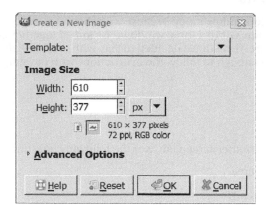

Figure 2-6. *In the Create New Image window, you can choose the size of your blank image.*

4. You can keep the height and width of the image at 610 × 377 pixels, or you can make the image larger or smaller by changing the numbers in the Width and Height area (see Figure 2-6).

5. For the adventurous, you can click on the Advanced Options and change the resolution to 300 pixels per inch. In the Comment area under Advanced Options, you can change "Created with GIMP" to "Created by a budding GENIUS."

6. Click OK.

Opening a Photo in GIMP

The image editing area is the place where you open images. The image editing area also contains GIMP's editing menus and more. It is not important what image you choose to open at this stage.

If you have never opened an image before, images are stored as files. You find images the same way you would find a Word document on your computer.

1. To open an image located on your computer, go to the menu bar located at the top of the Image window. In the File menu, click Open (see Figure 2-7).

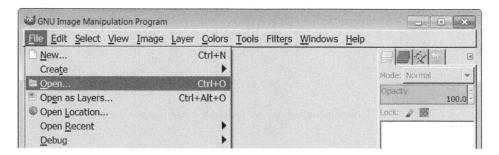

Figure 2-7. *To open an image, go to File, scroll down, and click Open.*

2. A pop-up menu shows your computer's folder structure. Search these folders for an image and then click Open. See Figure 2-8 for an example of a picture folder.

Usually images are stored in a Picture folder but you may have stored your images in another folder on your computer. Your folder and file system structure will probably look different than those in Figure 2-8; basically you are looking for an image on your hard drive. When you find an image to open, click Open, as shown in Figure 2-8.

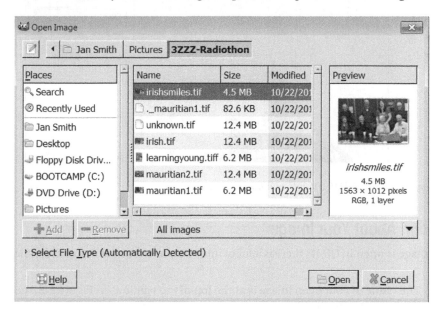

Figure 2-8. *Pop-up window in GIMP showing images in a Picture folder located on a hard drive. Different computer operating systems will have slightly different ways of displaying files located on your hard drive.*

3. You should now have an image open in the image editing area. Congratulations if you have progressed this far on your own. If you can't find your images on your computer, ask a friend to help you.

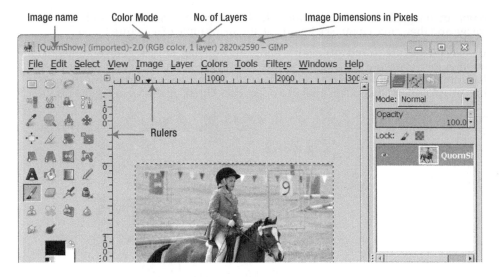

Figure 2-9. *Image open in GIMP's single-window mode workspace*

Information About Your Image

When an image is open in GIMP, there is a lot of information about the image available at a glance.

- The name of your open image is at the top of the window. In Figure 2-9, the name of the image is QuornShow.

- Color mode and Color/Index/Grayscale information is located at the top, next to the image name. In Figure 2-9, the color mode is RGB color. Don't worry if you are new to color modes; they are explained in Chapter 3.

- The number of layers the image has shows up at the top of the window. In Figure 2-9, QuornShow has one layer. You'll look at layers in Chapter 6.

- The dimensions of the open image are located at the top of the Image window. In Figure 2-9, the image dimensions are 2820 × 2590 pixels.

Rulers

The rulers are located at the top and one side of the image editing area, as you can see in Figure 2-9.

Rulers are useful to

- Understand the exact location of the mouse.

- Create accurate guides.

- Create sample points.

The default ruler measurement is in pixels. To change the unit of measurement for the rulers to other units, go to the drop-down list located on the bottom left of the workspace (see Figure 2-10). This is useful if you are going to print your image and want to see the size of your current image in inches or centimeters.

Guides

Guides are movable lines you can place vertically or horizontally over your picture to help line up items, visualize changes, etc. To place a guide on your image, drag your mouse from the side or top ruler into your image. This action will drag a guide onto the workspace (see Figure 2-10).

Guides can be handy when drawing or checking to see if the horizon in an image is level. You can drag the guide off the screen when not needed. To remove a guide, click the Move Tool and drag the guide back to the ruler (see Figure 2-10).

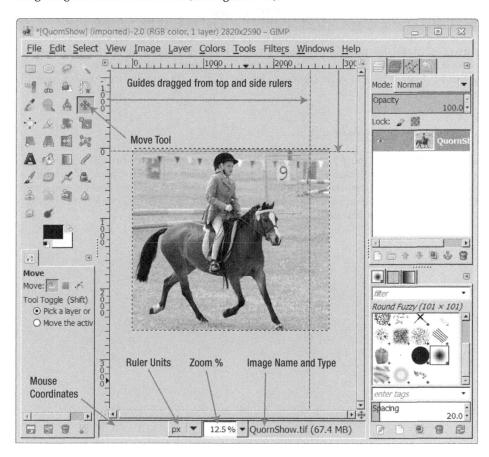

Figure 2-10. *Workspace showing ruler units, zoom options, guides and the Move Tool.*

25

Mouse Coordinates

Once again, beginners may not need this option but it can be handy if you need to know precisely where your mouse is located so you can come back to that spot later. As you move your mouse or pointer across your workspace, you can read the exact mouse coordinates near the bottom left corner of the window. The units used are the same as for the rulers (see Figure 2-10).

Zoom

When GIMP opens your image, it adjusts the view of the image to fit the available space. As you work in GIMP you may want to zoom in to see how something looks at 100% or you may want to zoom out to see the whole picture on the screen. Zooming in or out on an image doesn't affect the final size of your image. It's just the view of the image you see on your screen. In the next chapter, we show you how to find the exact size of your image.

To zoom in or out of your image, at the bottom of the window click the tab with the percentage value and choose from the drop-down list of sizes (see Figure 2-10). You can also enter in a Zoom level in the text box. Some people prefer zooming by clicking on the image and using the mouse wheel to zoom in and out. Perhaps the easiest way to zoom is to click the numbers on your keyboard: 1 = 100%, 2= 200%, etc. In GIMP, there is often more than one way to do something.

Image Resize to Fit Window

Image Resize is a handy option many people miss. Clicking the Image Resize button will zoom the image to fill the editing area. (Your image may already be filling the editing area). If you look at the image in Figure 2-10, you can see it is not filling the editing area. Compare this to the image in Figure 2-11, which is filling the editing area. Notice that the percentage indicator in the bottom of the window lets you know the percentage of the zoom.

Click icon to expand image to fit window

Zoom up to 800%

Figure 2-11. *One of the Zoom options in GIMP.*

RAM Usage, Not File Size

This is not something that beginners need to worry about but just in case you are curious, GIMP tells you at a glance how much RAM you are using. Located at the bottom center of Figure 2-11, is the measurement (88.4 MB). This number indicates the amount of computer RAM the image is using at that moment. This is not an indication of the file size of the image. We show you in the next chapter where to check the size of your image.

Quick Quiz

How much do you remember about the GIMP's workspace? Try this short quiz.

1. How do you zoom in on an image?

2. Where are the dimensions of your image located?

3. Where do you change the unit of measurement for your rulers?

4. How do you drag guidelines over your image?

Toolbox

The Toolbox has tools for painting, drawing, and working on photos (see Figure 2-12). It contains

- Selection tools to identify and isolate an area to work on.

- Paint tools to add strokes to your image.

- Transform tools to alter the shape or area of an image. New to GIMP 2.8 is Cage Transform.

- Color tools to alter colors across a selection or image.

- Text tools to add text to an image.

- Cloning and healing tools.

- Path tools and reusable shapes, such as the Bezier curve—an advanced option.

Go to your Toolbox and roll your mouse over a tool. A small description for that tool will pop up.

■ **Note** If you can't see the Toolbox on your screen, use the keyboard shortcut Control+B to bring the Toolbox in view. For the Mac, use the shortcut Command+B.

To turn a tool off, click another tool in the Toolbox.

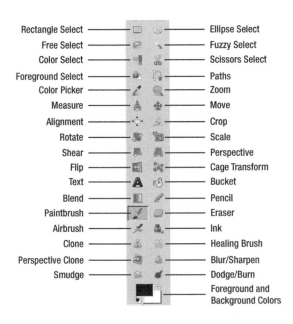

Rectangle Select	Ellipse Select
Free Select	Fuzzy Select
Color Select	Scissors Select
Foreground Select	Paths
Color Picker	Zoom
Measure	Move
Alignment	Crop
Rotate	Scale
Shear	Perspective
Flip	Cage Transform
Text	Bucket
Blend	Pencil
Paintbrush	Eraser
Airbrush	Ink
Clone	Healing Brush
Perspective Clone	Blur/Sharpen
Smudge	Dodge/Burn
	Foreground and Background Colors

Figure 2-12. The tools in the Toolbox. Roll your mouse over a tool to see its name and some information about it.

Open a blank image and experiment as you read on. It is probably obvious what the Brush, Pen, Ink, and Airbrush Tools do. However, you may not know that apart from a simple brush stroke, strokes can be made dynamic. This means the brush or pen responds to the speed you use your mouse or graphical tablet's pen. To turn on brush dynamics, select the brush tool in the Toolbox. In Tool Options, located below the Toolbox, click on the icon next to the word Dynamics. In the pop-up Dynamics menu, choose Basic Dynamics (see Figure 2-13). The Tool Options in the area below the Toolbox change with the selected tool.

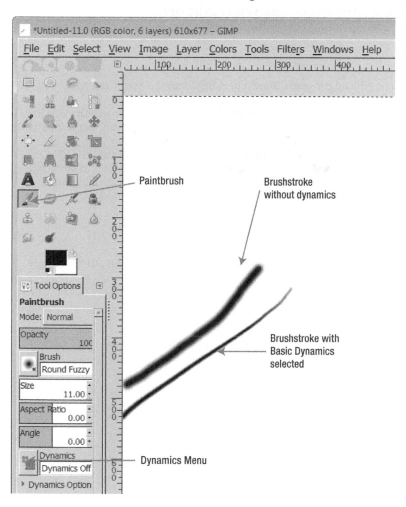

Figure 2-13. *The Paintbrush Tool options. Each tool has its own tool options located below the Toolbox.*

Quick Quiz

1. Can you name three ways of selecting part of an image?

2. What tool adds text to an image?

3. How many tools have brush-like strokes?

4. What tool do you use to remove or erase parts of an image?

Menus in GIMP

GIMP is a fully featured image editing program. Nowhere is this more evident than when you glance through GIMP's menus.

All GIMP's functionality can be accessed via the menu bar located at the top of the window in single-window mode. (If you are using GIMP's three separate windows, the menu bar is located at the top of the Image window).

Glance through the menu screenshots next to get an idea of the possibilities with GIMP. Some of the menu items will be obvious. However, the purpose of a number of menu items will not be obvious. We don't expect you to be an expert. When a menu item is needed later in the book, we show you when and—more importantly—where a menu item is located.

File Menu

The File menu is similar to File menus in many other programs (see Figure 2-14). In the File menu, you can

- **Open**, **create**, **save**, **save as**, and **export** images.

- **Open** recently closed images.

- **Create** or acquire a screenshot or an image from a camera or scanner.

- **Close** your images.

- **Quit** GIMP.

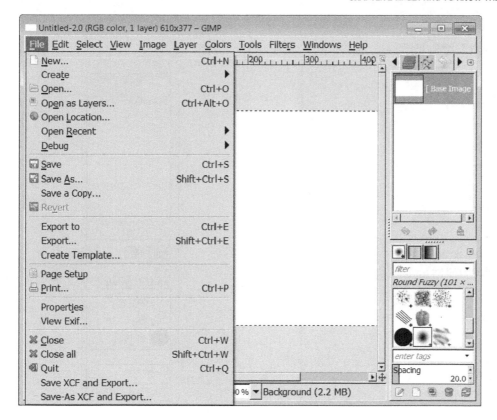

Figure 2-14. *The File menu is where you open, save, or export an image. It's also where you quit or exit GIMP.*

Edit Menu

The Edit menu has some very useful tools for beginners (see Figure 2-15). These are

- **Undo** or **Undo History** removes your last action; the Undo History Tab is useful when experimenting. (Control+Z will also undo your last action.)

- **Redo** restores your last action. (Control+Y will also redo your last action.)

- **Cut, copy,** and **paste**. (Control+C to copy and Control+V to paste; for Mac users, it is Command+C to copy and Command+V to paste)

- **Preferences** for GIMP are extensive and include boosting performance, setting up a graphics tablet, customizing the workspace, etc. Suggested preferences for beginners are in Chapter 10.

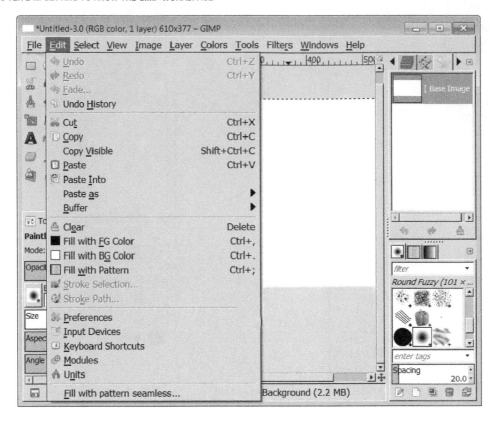

Figure 2-15. *The Edit menu*

It is worth trying Undo and Redo by going to Edit ➤ Undo. (Control+Z will also undo an action.)

Try also copy and paste. First, use a Tool from the Toolbox to select an area on an image, then go to Edit ➤ Copy, and then Edit ➤ Paste to paste it somewhere else on your image.

Select Menu

Many of the items in the Select menu are used on selected areas of an image (see Figure 2-16).

- **All** selects the whole image.

- **None** is useful when you wish to remove a selection.

- **Invert** reverses the current selection. Everything that was outside the selection is now included and vice versa.

- **Float** is a temporary layer; use a separate layer instead. Attach a floating layer to a layer before any editing can continue (Control-H). We explain this in full in Chapter 6.

- **Feather** softens a selection at its edges by blending into the surrounding pixels. You can choose how many pixels to feather.

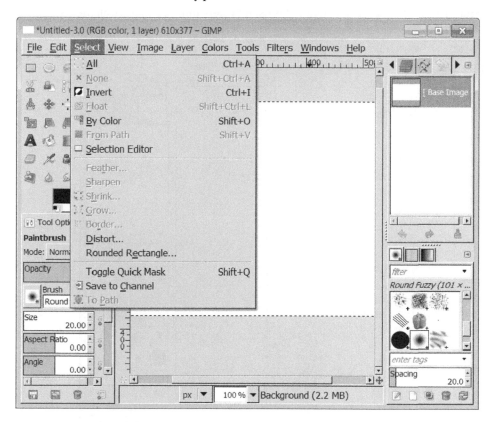

Figure 2-16. *The Select menu*

View Menu

For beginners, the View menu (Figure 2-17) offers a number of useful ways to view your image.

- **New View** makes another copy of your current image. This new view can be zoomed in or out. All editing affects both viewing copies. This is helpful when you are working on details in an image and at the same time need an overview of the image. Digital painters use this feature.

- **Dot for Dot** is useful for images for the web only. Please disable Dot for Dot for images intended for printing. You will see the images at their true size.

- **Zoom** gives options for zooming.

- **Show Grid** is a grid that will overlay your image. Use the grid to line up image elements.

- **Snap to Grid** works like a magnet. It is useful when lining up picture elements.

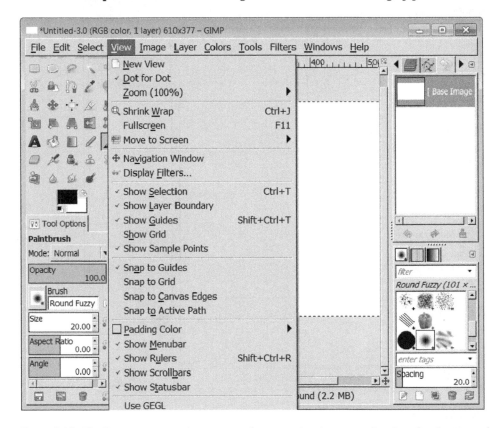

Figure 2-17. The View menu provides a range of ways to view images and options for showing rulers, guides, and selections.

Image Menu

The purpose of the Image menu (Figure 2-18) is to let you make some permanent decisions about your image.

- **Duplicate** makes an exact copy of your current image, including all layers, channels, and paths (the keyboard shortcut is Ctrl-D). Editing the duplicate image will not affect the original image.

- **Mode** changes the color mode of the image. Images in GIMP are RGB by default but it is possible to change the mode to Grayscale mode or Indexed color. An image with Indexed color only contains a limited set of colors and can be useful for graphics. The safest thing for beginners is to use RGB color.

- **Transform** will flip, rotate, or guillotine based on image guides.

- **Canvas Size** allows you to create extra space outside the image. This can be useful if you want to add text outside your image.

- **Print Size** allows you to change the resolution and dimensions of an image.

- **Scale Image** changes the number of pixels an image contains. Scaling up (making an image larger) loses quality.

- **Flatten Image** merges all layers. There is much more about layers and their uses in Chapter 6.

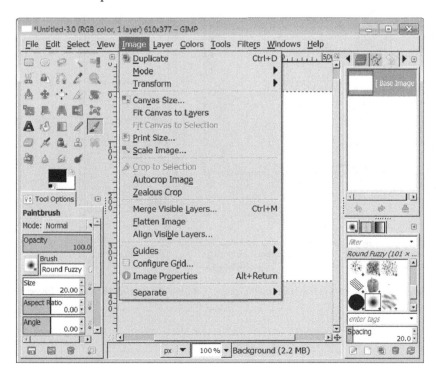

Figure 2-18. *The Image menu*

Layer Menu

You can skip this menu for now; layers are covered in Chapter 6. You will use layers when you add another image to your image, add text, create a montage, etc. However, if you're curious, the Layer menu contains layer management tools (see Figure 2-19).

- **New Layer** adds a new empty layer to your image, just above the active layer.

- **Duplicate Layer** adds a new layer, which is an exact copy of the active layer.

- **Delete Layer** deletes the active layer.

- **Stack** offers options to reorganize the layer order.

- **Mask** offers options to create, select, and apply a mask.

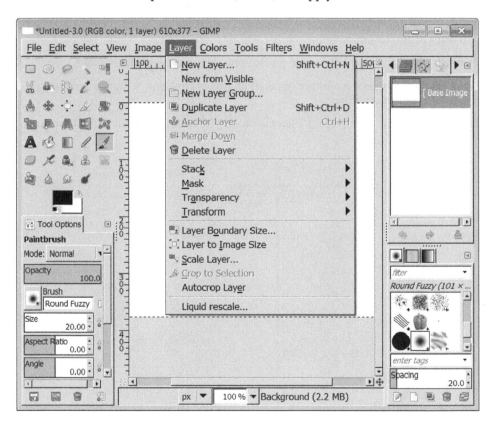

Figure 2-19. *The Layer menu is only useful when working with layers. Chapter 6 explains the uses for layers.*

Colors Menu

This area manages color. It has a range of tools to add snap and zing to images and drawings (see Figure 2-20). As beginners, you will learn how to use this menu when you work on optimizing or getting the best out of your images. Chapter 5 uses some of the options in the Colors menu for photographs. We also look at this menu in the chapters on drawing and painting.

- **Color Balance** increases or decreases the amount of cyan, magenta, or yellow in your image.

- **Hue-Saturation** is sliding scale to optimize the hue and saturation of your image.

- **Levels** controls shadows, midtones, and highlights in an image.

- **Curves** is a tool to change the color, brightness, and contrast of an image. Curves can bring life to a photo.

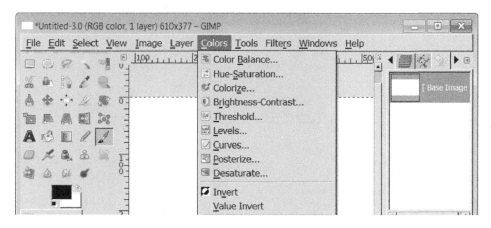

Figure 2-20. *The Colors menu*

Tools Menu

Most of the tools listed in this menu are also available from the Toolbox window located on the left of your screen in single-window mode. If you lose your Toolbox, press Ctrl+B and it will come to the top of your desktop. Alternatively, choose the tool from the Tools menu (see Figure 2-21). The letters opposite the Tool names in the menu are the keyboard shortcuts to select a tool.

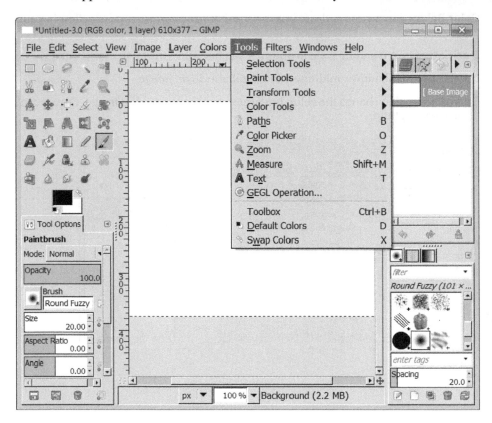

Figure 2-21. *The Tools menu provides an alternative way of selecting items usually accessed from the Toolbox. This can be useful if you have closed the Toolbox to create more screen space.*

Filters Menu

The filter section is one of the largest areas in GIMP (see Figure 2-22). You could spend days experimenting on your photos or drawings with the various filters here. In later chapters, we will work with filters.

The **Enhance** filters are important for beginners. These filters help improve imperfections of an original image such as lack of sharpness. The very useful but unhelpfully named Unsharp Mask is located at Filters ➤ Enhance ➤ Unsharp Mask.

The filters in this menu are available for the whole image, a layer, or a selection inside an image. How and when filters are applied is an individual choice. Open an image and try some of the filters. You will be amazed to see how much they can change your image.

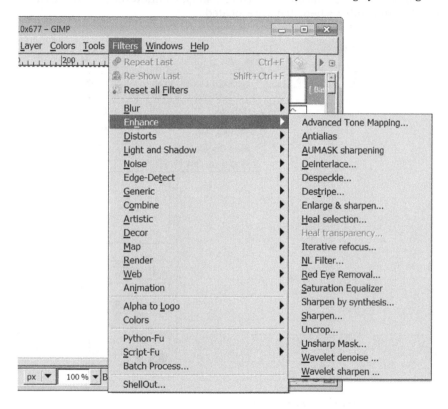

Figure 2-22. *The Filters menu*

Windows Menu

The Windows menu gives you access to a large range of dialogs or panels available in the Dockable Dialogs submenu (see Figure 2-23).

- Dockable Dialogs or Dockable Panels contain Layers, Undo, Paths, Brushes, Pallets, Gradients, and Fonts.

- **Single-Window Mode** is new to GIMP 2.8+. Scrolling down the Windows menu and clicking on "Single-Window Mode" joins the three separate GIMP windows together (it joins the Toolbox to the Image window and the Dialog or Panels window). If you are new to GIMP, we strongly recommend you try single-window mode. It makes it easier for you to remember where items are located.

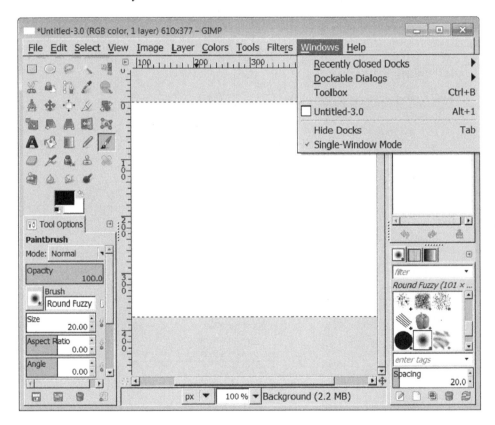

Figure 2-23. *The Windows menu*

Help Menu

The Help menu (Figure 2-24) offers additional resources and information.

- **GIMP Online** links to several GIMP web sites that provide additional free documentation and useful resources for users and developers. It is possible to download the Help and run it from your desktop.

- **About** offers information about the version of GIMP you have on your computer.

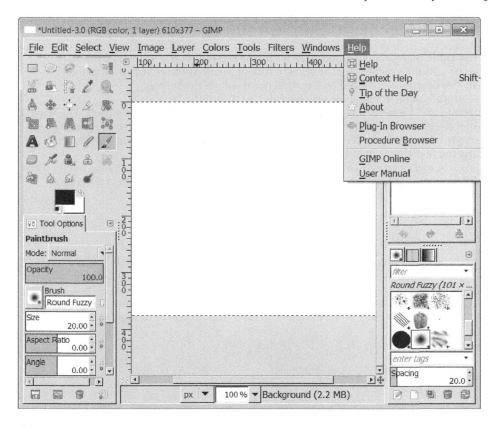

Figure 2-24. *The Help menu*

Alternative Ways to Access Menu Items

In GIMP, there is often more than one way to access a tool or an option. In the top menu bar you can access all the Toolbox tools when you click on Tools. The tools are also available in the Toolbox. To access the top menu bar items another way, right click with your mouse on the Image window screen and the main menu list appears.

Quick Quiz

1. How do you undo your last action?

2. Is Dot for Dot used for screen or print images?

3. Where are the image sharpening tools located?

4. What menu do you use to add a layer to an image?

Dockable Dialogs or Dockable Panels

GIMP offers dockable dialogs. But what is a dockable dialog? A dialog is a small box or window with a number of options available for the current tool or image such as a brush. In single-window mode, the dialogs are located on the right hand side of the screen.

The most useful dialog or panel for new users is the Undo History.

In other photo and image editing software, dialog docks are referred to as panels. There are a number of other dialogs or panels for Layers, Channels, etc. When GIMP first opens, on the right of your screen, you can see the Layers dialog and below this, the Brushes dialog (see Figure 2-25). There are many more dialogs out of sight.

(Each of the dialogs or panels can be dragged around the workspace to suit your needs. This option is really for experienced users. It is not useful to move dialogs around before you are comfortable with the whole GIMP workspace.)

Undo History—Great for Beginners

The Undo History is by far one of the most useful dialogs or panels for beginners. On the top far right of your screen, click on the curved yellow arrow to reveal your undo history. If you can't see the yellow arrow, drag the far right edge of your workspace to reveal the area.

In Figure 2-25, Undo History is selected and you should be able to see a four-step rough drawing of an eye. Clicking on any of those steps will undo that image to that point.

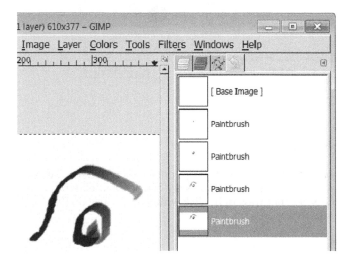

Figure 2-25. *Clicking on the yellow curved arrow opens the Undo History area.*

Quick Quiz

1. What is a dialog or panel?

2. Where is your image's Undo History area?

Summary

This chapter was a tour through GIMP's workspace. We looked at GIMP's three workspace windows: the Toolbox, the Image window, and the Dockable Dialogs window. To make things easier to find, we joined these three windows into single-window mode. You saw how to open an image and view the information available at a glance about that image. We listed and explored some of the Tools in the Toolbox. We toured through the menu area. In the Dockable Dialogs area, we looked at dialogs and how to find the Undo History area. We included four quizzes to help you move through this material.

■ ■ ■

CHAPTER 3

Basic Computer Graphics

In This Chapter:

- Choosing a file format for your Image

- Image Resolution

- Preparing Images for the Internet

- Preparing Images for Printing

Digital images appear in advertisements, in newspapers, magazines, the Internet and on television. The relatively low cost of digital imaging has enabled more and more people to explore their creativity via digital art. It has been possible for some time to print your digital images or upload them to the Internet. Now your digital images can go onto business cards, calendars, clothing, drink coasters, flags, flyers, key rings, logos, mouse mats, mugs, newsletters, placemats, rulers etc. The places where images appear seems to grow each year, no space is too small, too large or too obscure.

It is possible to download photos from your digital camera and have them printed to your medium immediately. However, there comes a time for many people when they want more control over the look of their images. GIMP gives you control over the size, shape and exposure of an image. It allows you to add text, other images or parts of an image and many other creative concepts. In fact, you probably feel like jumping to a later chapter and doing something creative right now. If you are a beginner, please answer these questions first. Do you know what digital resolution is? Do you know when to use low resolution images and when to use high resolution images? Do you know the most appropriate file type for your digital project? Do you know how to save an image in GIMP? If you are not sure about any of these questions, keep reading this chapter.

Choosing an Image File Format

Choosing the correct file format for your image is one of the most important things you can do to ensure your image displays well and is available, in good condition, for future reuse.

GIMP works with a large number of image file formats. Here is a list of the most common file formats available in GIMP.

Suggested File Types for Beginners

For beginners and those in a hurry, you can get by using two file types, XCF and JPG. Save the work you are editing as an XCF file. When you have finished editing, export your image as a JPG. It is worth noting that GIMP saves files by default to the XCF file format. This is a good thing because your image is saved to a format which helps you avoid some errors beginners often make. To save an image to another file format the image is exported. We explain the simple procedure for exporting images later in this chapter.

Why not save the file as a JPG and forget about XCF you may say. Read the paragraph on JPG below, to find out why that is not a good idea.

JPG

JPG or JPEG is a very popular format for images. If you are downloading files from your camera or phone, your image files most likely have .jpg at the end of them. JPG images get compressed in the camera to reduce the file size.

It is a very good idea to make a copy of your JPG image *before* you start editing. Many people do not realize that each time a JPG image is saved there will be some loss of quality. This loss of quality is permanent.

JPG files are ideal to use on the Internet because it is possible to reduce the file size of a JPG when you are saving an image. Smaller files sizes make web pages open faster. Later this chapter explains how to save (Export) a JPG image.

Some beginners compromise on quality by choosing a camera setting which allows the largest number of JPG images for their card. Once information is reduced in size, it gives little room to move when you may want to tweak your colors or contrast in image editing software.

GIF

GIF is a low quality file format used for graphics with very few colors (256 colors). GIF can be useful for simple animation on the web. A better choice for web graphics is PNG.

PNG

PNG (Portable Network Graphic) replaces the GIF file format for graphics on the web. Why is PNG better than GIF? PNG supports a greater range of transparency and handles a much larger range of colors. PNG has better file compression than GIF. However, PNG does not support animation.

PSD

GIMP can open and save Photoshop PSD files. It is possible to edit each layer separately in GIMP, save it as a PSD and then open it in Photoshop. However, PSD images opened in GIMP that have had Adjustment Layers applied to them in Photoshop will not show up in GIMP. A PSD image created in GIMP will open in Photoshop without problems. PSD is comparable in complexity to XCF the native file format for GIMP.

RAW

RAW files are available from higher end digital cameras. RAW files are larger than JPG files because they contain a lot more information about your image. The advantage of RAW files (unlike JPG files) is that the image is preserved in an uncompressed format. RAW files give you a greater control over the dynamic range of your image, that is the range from the brightest part of the image to the darkest part of the image. White Balance can be changed in a RAW image. RAW files also contain the Meta Data belonging to the image. Meta Data includes such things as the time and date the image was taken, the camera make and model, the camera settings such as the F stop and speed and if available it will also record the GPS location.

In GIMP for MAC, RAW files open via an already installed plugin called UFRaw. Windows users will need to install the UFRaw Plugin (see Chapter 10) or convert RAW files to TIF before opening them in GIMP. Linux users may have to also install UFRaw to open RAW files.

Once a RAW file is opened in GIMP it cannot be saved back as a RAW file. Once a RAW image has been worked on in GIMP it can be exported as a JPG for web or printing work. If saving/exporting to JPG make sure the quality is set to high. An opened RAW file can be exported as a TIF, this can be a good option if you are working with large file sizes for images to be printed. If you hit Save in GIMP the RAW file will be saved as an XCF file. This is a good option if you intend to do more work on the image.

TIF

TIF (Tagged Image File Format) is a high quality format. TIF files are larger than JPG files. TIF use a lossless compression format. This means if you save a few times, while working on the image, it does not lose quality. TIF is a popular file format for printing, scanning and archiving images.

XCF

XCF is the GIMP native file format. This format stores all of the data making up your image. XCF saves your image layers, guides, transparency, paths and active channels and meta data. This file format is the recommended file format to use in GIMP when editing your images.

XCF files are for use within GIMP only. When you have finished editing an image, the final step is to export (save) the image to another file format. You can export an XCF image to a JPG for the web or TIF for printing or to any of the other file formats supported in GIMP. Exporting is explained later in this chapter.

This format does not save your Undo History. No file format saves your undo history in GIMP. Save progressive versions of your image if you think you may need to roll back to an earlier state.

Quick Quiz

1. Name two advantages with JPG images

2. Why does a JPG lose quality every time you open and edit an image?

3. What is the best file format for extensive editing in GIMP?

■ **Tip** To improve the quality of your digital images, check your digital camera manual, to see if your camera can take RAW images. A RAW image contains all the digital metadata about the image. GIMP can open RAW image with the aid of a Plugin called UFRaw. For example, there is the ability to change the white balance, to increase the dynamic range or to recover better from an overly dark or overly bright image. RAW files are larger than JPG files.

Zooming in GIMP

The size of the image you see on your computer screen does not necessary mean that is the actual size of the image. Check that you are zoomed at 100%. Zoom changes your view of the image on your screen.

There are many ways to zoom in GIMP:

- Zoom by typing these numbers on your keyboard: 1 to zoom 100%, 2 to zoom 200%, 3 to zoom 400%, 4 to zoom 800%.

- Zoom via the menu options in View ➤ Zoom.

- Zoom using the Magnifying Tool located in the Tool Box.

- Zoom via the pull-down menu at the bottom edge of the workspace window.

- Keyboard Shortcuts for Zooming:

  - Fit Image in Window Shift +Ctrl+E

  - Zoom In +

  - Zoom Out –

When editing a digital image it is a good practice to zoom to 100% or greater. This is particularly useful if you are editing a small area of an image.

Image Basics

It is sensible to start digital editing with some good work practices. Beginners often disregard any thought about image resolution until it bites them. For example, a beginner may have an image uploaded to a website and people have commented favorably about the image. One day the beginner decides to make a very large print of this image and hang it on a wall. They are horrified to see that the printed image is fuzzy. It is not good enough to hang on a wall. Why did this happen? The short answer is the only copy of the image was optimized for the Internet. We will guide you to avoid disasters like this.

Make a Copy of Your Image

Before you start editing an image, we recommend you work on a copy of your original image. There are a few reasons for this.

- You might make a mistake and ruin your only copy

- You might make your only copy smaller to fit on a web page. Thus making the only copy of your image, smaller and lesser in quality

- Opening, editing and saving a JPG image many times will deteriorate the quality of the image.

- Disk space is relatively cheap compared to going back and taking that special photo again.

The easiest way to make another copy of your image is save it as an XCF file. XCF is GIMP's high quality native file format. This means you keep the same name as the original but it has a different file ending. For example, myimage.jpg could be the original and myimage.xcf. could be the copy of the original.

Save Your Work

Don't forget to save as your work as you go, rather than at the end of the entire editing process. Save your working copy in GIMP's native file format .xcf. The .xcf file retains quality, and preserves layers, if you are using them. When the editing is complete, you can save the image as a JPG or TIF or the recommended file for your project. Some people protest that saving images as .xcf files, uses too much disk space. We are recommending this only for the images you do extensive work on not for every image you own. If you have invested an hour or so editing a special image, we think you should retain the best quality for that image.

Save Your Image as an XCF File

Saving your image as an XCF file, preserves quality as you work on your image. You have the choice later to export the image to a JPG or any other image file type.

1. Open an image in GIMP by going to File ➤ Open, see Figure 3-1.(see Chapter 2 if you are unsure)

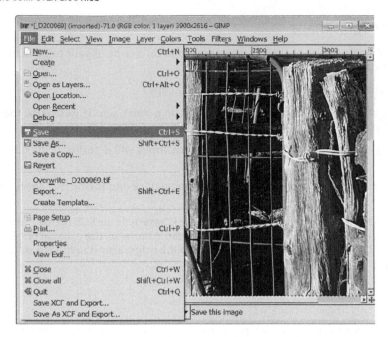

Figure 3-1. *GIMP's File Menu*

2.   To save the image as an xcf file, go to File ➤ Save, see Figure 3-2.

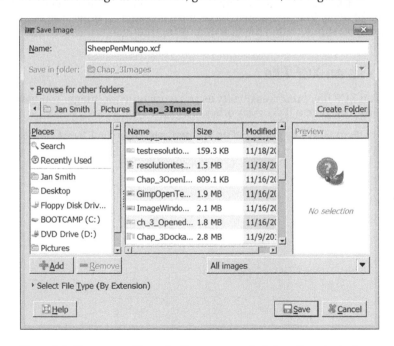

Figure 3-2. *Name your file in the Name area and click on Save in the bottom right corner*

What Is Image Resolution?

When taking photos, choose the highest resolution your camera will allow. This will give you the best quality and the biggest file size. You can always reduce the size of the image later.

So what is image resolution? Digital images have thousands and thousands of tiny pixels. Figure 3-3 shows pixels enlarged many times, normally you cannot see the actual pixels. The number of pixels per inch (ppi) determines resolution. In other words, the resolution is the number of pixels along the width and height of an image. The more pixels packed together per inch the higher the resolution, similarly the fewer pixels per inch the lower the resolution.

When you edit an image in GIMP or any other digital image editor, you are editing pixels. Pixels are tiny elements storing variations of brightness and color. The word pixel is an amalgamation of the words picture and element. GIMP edits pixels by coloring, shading, counting, selecting, moving, blending or removing pixels.

Figure 3-3. *An extreme close up of individual pixels*

■ **Note** For geeks only, the digital images GIMP edits are raster images. Raster images are made up of pixels. Another type of digital image is the vector image. Vector images use geometrical points, lines and curves to represent images. GIMP can open a vector image and export it as a raster image but GIMP cannot export the image as a vector image. The one exception is that GIMP Paths can export to SVG, which is a vector graphics format. If you are looking for an open source vector image editor, try Inkscape.

It is difficult to see the individual pixels in the image in Figure 3-4, because the resolution is high. The blossom image has a resolution of 300ppi. Its pixel measurements are 1056 × 755 pixels or 804,075 pixels.

Figure 3-4. *This image has a high resolution of 300 ppi (pixels per inch)*

■ **Note** Image Resolution is measured in ppi. The term ppi stands for the number of pixels per inch. An image with 300ppi is a high resolution image. An image with 72ppi is a low resolution image.

You may hear people refer to dpi – this stands for dots per inch. dpi refers to the resolution of a printer. A printer with a resolution of 1200 dpi should print good copies of images saved at 300ppi. A printer with a resolution of 400dpi would give a less satisfactory result. The reason being a printer printing 1200dpi is printing many more dots per inch compared to a printer with a resolution of 400dpi which is only printing 400 dots per inch.

Comparing Image Resolution

Figure 3-5, has two versions of the same image. However, the images have different resolutions. The image on the left in Figure 3-5 has a resolution of 300 ppi. This is a high resolution image. The image on the right in Figure 3-5 has a resolution of 72 ppi. Although the image on the right has a poorer quality on the printed page, on a computer screen it would appear normal. Images for the web will load faster the smaller the file size. An image with a low resolution will have a smaller file size than the same image with a high resolution.

Figures 3-5a and 3-5b. *The image on the left has a resolution of 300 ppi and a file size of 1 MB. The image on the right has been scaled to a resolution of 72 ppi and a file size of 50 KB.*

Quick Quiz

1. What does ppi stand for?
2. What resolution should you save an image for the Internet?
3. What resolution should you save an image to be printed?

Checking Image Resolution in GIMP

As mentioned, an image with a high resolution will have more pixels than a low resolution image with the same height and width.

To check the resolution of your image:

1. In the top menu, go to File ➤ Open. (for further information on opening an image, see Chapter 2).

2. To see the image resolution and other properties for your image in GIMP, go to the Image Menu ➤ Image Properties. See Figure 3-6. Scroll down and click on Image Properties at the bottom of the list, as shown in Figure 3-6.

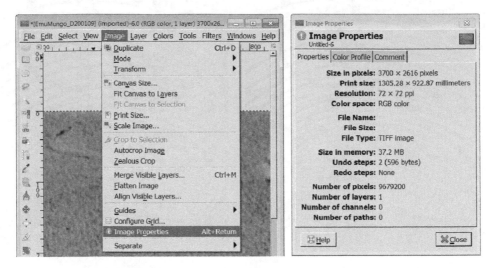

Figure 3-6. *On the left, Image Properties is selected, on the right the pop-up Image Properties dialog showing a resolution of 72 ppi and other information about the image*

3. A pop-up panel or screen will appear showing the image properties for the open image. See the Image Properties dialog on the right in Figure 3-6.

Resolution for Printed Images

Printed images need a high resolution, 300 ppi is a recommended resolution for printed images. When you change the image resolution, the following occurs:

- Decreasing the resolution means the width and height of an image increases. This happens because you are assigning fewer pixels per inch so the images expands in size.

- Increasing the resolution, means the width and height of an image decreases. This is because you are squeezing in more pixels in per inch.

When saving (File ➤ Export in GIMP) an image for printing, choose a resolution of 300 ppi. Export the image as a TIF file. TIF files are a high quality option.

To Increase or Decrease Resolution

To change the resolution of your image:

1. Go to the top menu click on the Image menu and scroll down and click on Print Size. See Figure 3-7.

2. In the pop-up Set Image Print Resolution dialog, in the resolution box change the resolution, then click OK.

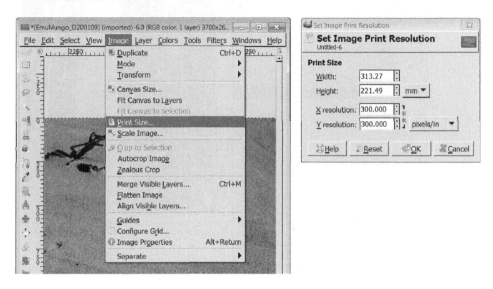

Figure 3-7. *To change the resolution go to Image* ➤ *Print Size and change the resolution in the Set Image Print Resolution dialog*

Saving a JPG, PNG, PSD, and TIF File in GIMP

Unlike most software programs GIMP 2.8 saves most image files via the File ➤ Export Menu not File ➤ Save. File ➤ Save is only used for GIMP's native file format XCF.

Saving Files in GIMP via the File ➤ Export Menu

To save a JPG, PNG, PSD, TIF or other file in GIMP:

1. Click on the File menu.

2. Scroll down and click on Export. See Figure 3-8.

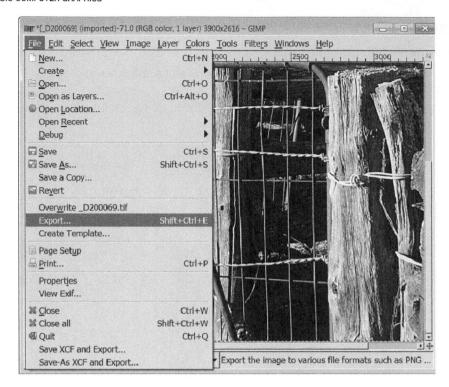

Figure 3-8. *Save JPG, GIF, PNG, PSD, and TIF files via the Export menu not the Save menu*

3. In the Export Image window, check the correct name for your file. See Figure 3-9.

4. In the Export Image window, choose a folder to save your image. Either choose a folder from the folders shown in the 'Save in folder' drop down list. Alternatively, browse for the correct folder by clicking on the + next to Browse for other folders. See Figure 3-9.

5. Choose a file by clicking on the small arrow next to Select File_Type (By Extension). See Figure 3-9.

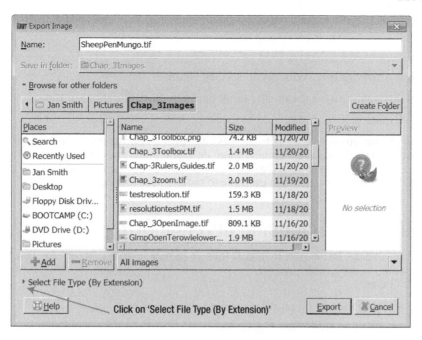

Figure 3-9. *The Export Image pop-up window. Click on the + next to Select File_Type (By Extension). A list of file choices will open.*

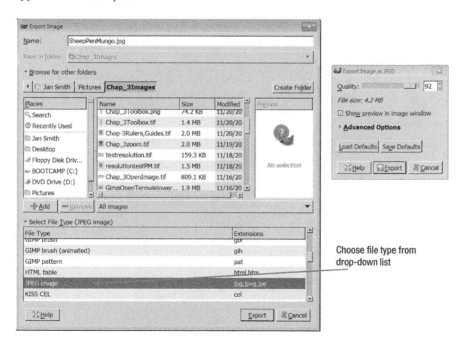

Figure 3-10. *Scroll down and select JPEG, the pop-up Export Image as JPEG will appear.*

6. From the list, select the image file format, the example has JPG selected. See Figure 3-10.

7. Click on Export.

8. A pop-up Export Image as JPEG Window opens. See Figure 3-10.

9. For a good quality image, move the quality slider between the numbers 92 to 100.

10. Then Click on Export

If you intend to upload your image to a website such as eBay or the photographic website Flickr, take a note of your file size. If your file is smaller than 5MB, you image will up load ok. Flickr can take files up to 10MB. If however your file size is larger than this or you need your image as part of a web design, move onto the next example to reduce your file size further.

Saving (Exporting) and Reducing JPG File Size

The difference between this and the last exporting task is that we reduce the file size further. This is done by taking an extra step in the Export process.

To save or (export) an image:

1. Go to the File ➤ Export menu.(If you are unsure refer to Figure 3-8).

2. The Export Image window opens. See Figure 3-11.

3. Type the name for your file, in the Name area, see Figure 3-11.

4. Select a folder to save your image in.

5. Choose a file type by clicking on the the small arrow next to Select File_Type (By Extension). See Figure 3-11.

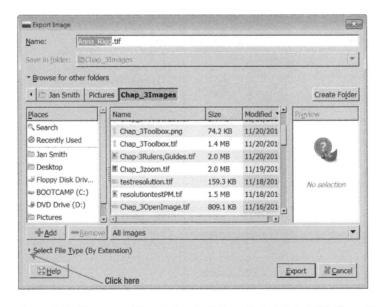

Figure 3-11. *The pop-up Export Image dialog, click on Select File Type (By Extension)*

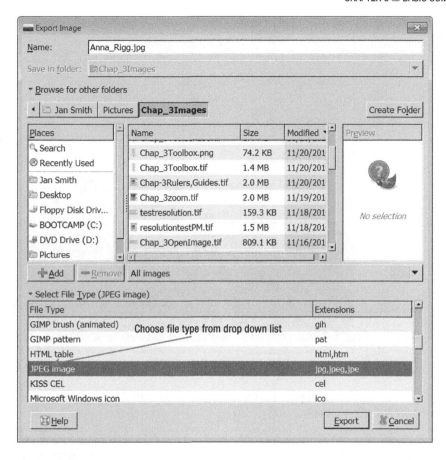

Figure 3-12. *In the drop down list of files choose JPG Image*

6. Scroll down and choose JPG. See Figure 3-12.

7. In the pop-up 'Export my Image as a JPG' window, click the checkbox next to 'Show preview in image window'. This allows you to see the effects on your image of reducing the file size. See Figure 3-13.

8. Make sure you are viewing your image at 100% (Press the number 1 on your keyboard to zoom to 100%).

9. Use the Quality slider in the Pop-up window, Export Image as JPEG, to reduce the file size of your image, see Figure 3-13.

10. Click on Export in the pop-up window when you are happy with the file size and the look of the image.

Figure 3-13. *Exporting or Saving a JPG image for the Internet. Use the Quality slider to reduce the file size of your image.*

Once you have exported an image in GIMP, you can use Control E to update the file. GIMP remembers where you exported the file. Alternatively, you can go to File ➤ Export As to update the image.

■ **Caution** Settings in GIMP such as Zoom and Dot for Dot changes your view of an image on your screen it is not permanent. To permanently change the size of an image, the image is scaled in the Image ➤ Scale Image menu. Disable Dot for Dot by going to the View menu and unchecking Dot for Dot.

Summary

We highlighted some traps for beginners when they start saving images. We discussed the importance of image resolution and file size in determining the successful outcome of a digital project. The major image file types were discussed to help choose the best file type for your project. We showed you the slightly quirky way to save images in GIMP. With some sensible basic information under your belt, it is now time to edit your images.

CHAPTER 4

■ ■ ■

Image Straightening, Cropping, Scaling, and Perspective

In This Chapter

- Rotating or cropping an image

- Making an image larger or smaller

- Fixing leaning buildings and other perspective work

- Applying different frames to your image

In this chapter we will show you how to add a frame or border to your image and how to crop and resize an image. We will also show you how to straighten an image and correct perspective distortion. Most importantly, we show you where to find these options in GIMP. Table 4-1 gives an overview of the tasks in the chapter. We don't expect you to work through every exercise, choose the tasks that interest you. This way you will have more fun.

Table 4-1. *Straightening, Cropping, Scaling, Perspective, and Framing*

Image Problem	GIMP Solution	GIMP Location
Does the image need straightening?	Rotate Tool	Rotate Tool is located in the Toolbox
Is the image upside down?	Transform	Menu Image ➤ Transform ➤ Flip Vertically
Is the image untidy? Does it have distracting elements near the edges?	Crop Tool	Crop Tool is located in the Toolbox

Continued

Image Problem	GIMP Solution	GIMP Location
Is the image too small?	Image Resize Tool	Menu Image ➤ Scale Image
Is the image too big? Does the image need smaller dimensions for use on a web site?	Image Resize Tool	Menu Image ➤ Scale Image
Is there a perspective problem in the image? Is it marred by a leaning building?	Perspective Tool	Perspective Tool is located in the Toolbox
Would you like to add a frame or border to your image?	Several options available	Menu Filters ➤ Décor

Straightening or Rotating an Image

An image might be horizontally or vertically crooked. This is a very common task and an easy one for a beginner.

To Straighten an Image

1. Open an image by going to the menu at the top of the screen, File ➤ Open. (See Chapter 2 if you need help opening an image.)

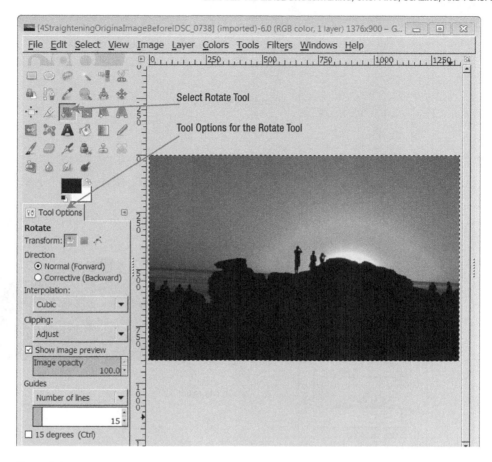

Figure 4-1. *The horizon in this image is not level.*

2. Go to the Toolbox and click on the Rotate Tool (Figure 4-1).

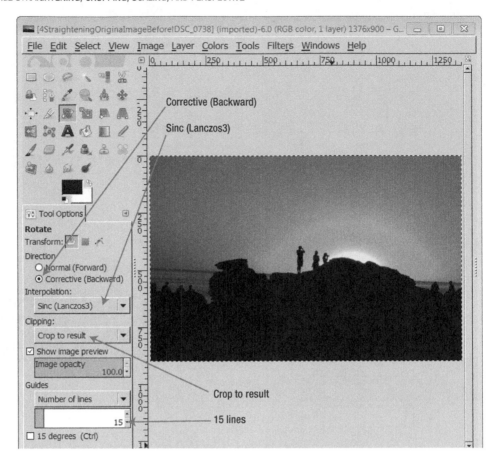

Figure 4-2. *Options for the Rotate Tool*

3. In the Rotate Tool options (Figure 4-2), set the following:

- Under Direction, select Corrective (Backward).

- (Optional) For Interpolation choose Cubic or Sinc (Lanczos3).

- Under Clipping, select Crop to result.

- Under Guides: Number of lines for grid, select 15. You may find you want more or less lines in your grid.

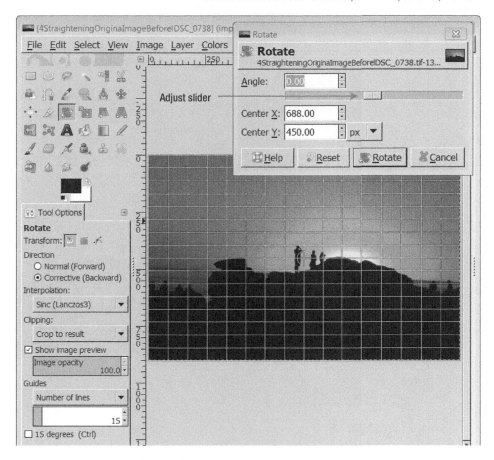

Figure 4-3. *The Rotate Tool with the grid over the image*

4. Click on the image. The grid is on top of the image, as you can see in Figure 4-3.

5. In the Rotate dialog, adjust the slider to line up the horizon with the grid. See Figure 4-3.

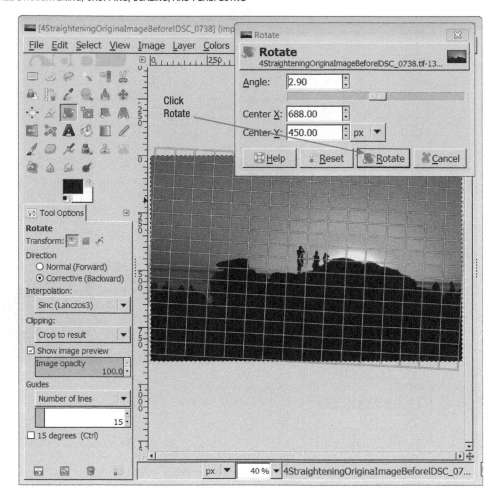

Figure 4-4. *Rotating the image*

6.   When you line up your image to the grid, click Rotate, as shown in Figure 4-4.

Figure 4-5. *Image is now straight but it has blank space around the edges.*

7. The image is corrected but it has empty space around the edge (see Figure 4-5).

8. To remove the empty space around the image, go to Image ➤ Autocrop Image (see Figure 4-6).

Figure 4-6. *Choose Image ➤ Autocrop Image to remove the blank space around the outside of the image.*

■ **Tip** Saving Files Is Slightly Different in GIMP. An unusual design feature of GIMP 2.8 is that only GIMP's native file XCF is saved via File ➤ Save. File formats (such as JPG, TIF, PNG, PSD, etc.) are saved by going to File ➤ Export. See Chapter 3 for further details.

Image Opens Upside Down

From time to time an image may open upside down in GIMP. For example, an image might appear upside down if it was scanned that way.

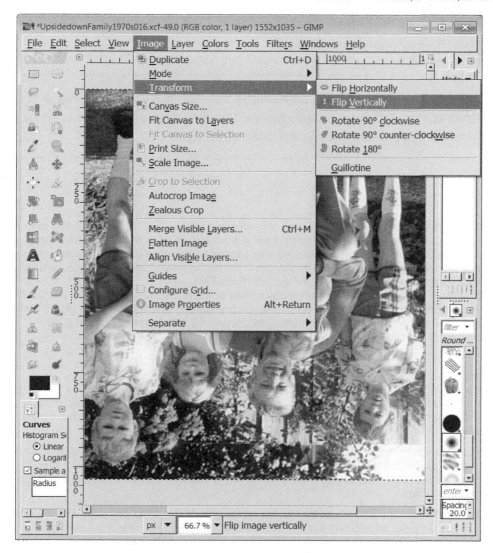

Figure 4-7. *Flip or rotate an image with Image ➤ Transform.*

To Flip an Image Vertically

1. Go to Image ➤ Transform (Figure 4-7).

2. Select Flip Vertically. Your image will turn 180 degrees.

The Image Menu has a range of ways to turn your image in the Transform menu. You can

- Flip horizontally

- Flip vertically

- Rotate 90 degrees clockwise
- Rotate 90 degrees counterclockwise

■ **Tip** The screenshots in this book use GIMP's single-window mode. We recommend single-window mode for beginners as it joins the three workspaces together. To move to single-window mode, in the top menu go to Windows ➤ Single-Window Mode. Further details are in Chapter 2.

Cropping an Image

Often the only improvement a photo needs is a little cropping. When you crop a photo, you are removing some of the original edges from the photo. Cropping is useful to remove distracting items and to make the photo more artistic or pleasing. Cropping an image can sometimes turn an ordinary image into something special. No matter what the reason, if you are unhappy with the framing of your image, one solution is to use the GIMP Crop Tool.

Before cropping, make a copy of your image by saving or exporting the image (see Chapter 2 if you need a refresher). Decide before you crop how you are going to use this image (print or web site), then set the correct resolution. (See Chapter 3 for further information about setting the correct resolution for your image).

Basic Crop

In this example, you can select any part of your image to crop. This means the image will change its shape and dimensions. If you need to crop to a specific width or to an aspect ratio, move on to the next exercise.

1. Select the Crop Tool in the Toolbox (see Figure 4-8). The Crop Tool is located in the Toolbox on the left of the screen if you are in single-window mode. If you have the default layout and can't see the Toolbox, use the keyboard shortcut Control+B to bring up the Toolbox.

2. To help decide where to crop, use Golden sections from the drop-down list. (see Figure 4-8) The Golden sections will display over your image when you select the photo with your mouse. (Golden sections are a variation on a long-standing photographic idea, the rule of thirds. The guide divides a photo horizontally and vertically into thirds. Some people say the eye more naturally goes to points of interest located in these divisions rather than the center of an image.)

3. To start selecting, drag the mouse diagonally across the image.

4. To align the crop selection more accurately, the selected area has a square box in each corner of the selection. Drag the mouse inside any of those square borders to make your crop selection larger or smaller (see Figure 4-8).

5. To crop the image, press Enter. Figure 4-9 shows the result.

Figure 4-8. *The highlighted area is to kept in the crop.*

Figure 4-9. *The photo has been cropped using the cropping tools in GIMP.*

■ **Note** Have you ever noticed that the framing of your image does not always turn out the way you expected? If you use a point-and-shoot camera, the framing of the scene you see in the camera is not accurate. Viewfinders in point-and-shoot cameras give an approximation of the framing of the image you are taking. The viewfinder is usually located above and to one side of the lens. In contrast, DSLR cameras have through-the-lens viewing so it's much easier to frame a shot.

Cropping to an Aspect Ratio

The aspect ratio is the relationship between the length and width of an image. In the excitement to work on a photo, it is easy to overlook the fact that the aspect ratio of your image may be different from the aspect ratio where your edited image will be displayed. You may display your images on a screen, a digital photo frame, or as a printed photograph. Each of these display media has aspect ratios that may be different from the aspect ratio of your image. These discrepancies are described in the following two sections. The instructions for cropping to an aspect ratio follow these sections.

Displaying Images in a Digital Photo Frame

If you display your images in a digital photo frame, the frame may have a different aspect ratio from your camera's aspect ratio. If the aspect ratios don't match, your digital photo frame might compensate in ways that might not be visually pleasing. The digital photo frame may crop your image automatically, thereby cutting off vital parts of the picture. It may stretch your image to fit the frame, thus distorting your image or it may have a black line down two sides of your image.

Check the Photo Size before Printing

The aspect ratio of an image produced by a camera doesn't match the aspect ratio of most photo paper. This absolute silliness was the case in the film camera days and is still the case today. In simple terms, the image produced by your camera has a different width-to-height ratio than most photo paper.

If you are printing an image, it makes sense to crop your image to the same aspect ratio as the paper the photo is printed on. If you don't crop or resize your image, the image is usually cropped automatically in the printing process. This might not be a pleasant surprise. An Australian friend of ours worked on her European holiday images in a digital editor. To her horror, when the images were printed, important parts of many images were cropped out in the printing process. She did not know why this had happened and was very upset. No one had told her to check the paper sizes in use at the printing shop.

■ **Tip** When printing your images, set your resolution to 300 ppi. See Chapter 3 for more details.

Cropping to an Aspect Ratio in GIMP

There may be times when you need to crop an image to a specific ratio. For example, a ratio of 6:4 is a common size for small printed photos.

1. Select the Crop Tool in the Toolbox (see Figure 4-10). The Crop Tool is located in the Toolbox on the left of the screen if you are in single-window mode. If you can't see the Toolbox, use the keyboard shortcut Control+B to bring up the Toolbox.

2. The Crop Tool has a Tool Options box that is located below the Toolbox.

3. Choose Aspect ratio from the drop-down list next to the checkbox.

4. In the Tool Options, select "Fixed" next to Aspect ratio.

5. Type in the Aspect ratio you need. (The example in Figure 4-10 has a ratio of 6:4.)

6. To start the selection process, drag the mouse diagonally across the image. (This can be an approximate selection.)

7. To align the crop selection more accurately, the selected area has a square box in each corner of the selection. Drag the mouse inside any of those square borders to make your crop selection larger or smaller.

8. To crop the image, press Enter. Figure 4-11 shows the result.

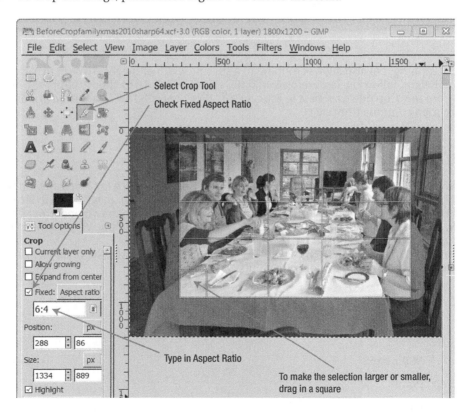

Figure 4-10. *Selecting aspect ratio in the Crop Tool options area*

73

Figure 4-11. *Image cropped to 6:4 ratio*

Cropping to a Width or Height

GIMP's cropping tool also allows cropping to a specific width or height. To crop to a specific width or height, follow the last exercise until the end of step 2. Then choose either the height or width from the drop down list next to aspect ratio. (See Figure 4-10.) Type the height or width in the box, then continue from step 6.

Changing the Size of an Image

You may need to change the size or dimensions of an image, perhaps for a web site or for printing. It is possible to scale an image smaller or larger. Scaling an image down in size usually doesn't affect the quality of the image. Making an image larger than the original can affect image quality. It is a good practice to make a copy of your image before scaling. When you have saved (or exported) your scaled image, the change is permanent.

The Scale Image option in GIMP allows you to make an image smaller or larger. You can scale your image by one of the following units:

- Pixels
- Percentage
- Inches
- Millimeters
- Points
- Pica

For the following exercises, we suggest you avoid using the scale tool in the Toolbox. This example uses the Scale Image option located in the Image menu (Image ➤ Scale Image). There is often more than one way of doing things in GIMP. We show the most useful tools, rather than every possible way to do a task.

■ **Tip** Scaling is quite different from zooming. When you zoom in or out of an image on your screen, this just affects the view you see on the screen. Zoom does not permanently change your image size. Scaling changes your image permanently to another size.

Making an Image Larger

If you make an image larger (in other words, if you scale up an image), there may be some loss of quality to the image in the process. The amount of loss of quality when enlarging depends on the quality of the image and the amount of the enlarging. When enlarging an image, the interpolation tool adds extra pixels.

GIMP's Scale Image area sets the size of any image you open at 100%. To double an image in size, choose 200%. Experiment with different percentages to see what works for your image.

To make an image larger or to scale up an image, follow these steps:

1. Go to Image ➤ Scale Image (see Figure 4-12).

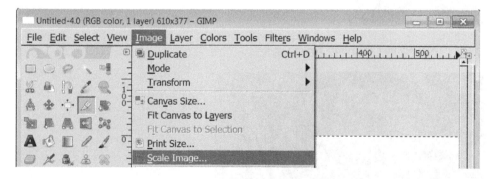

Figure 4-12. Choose Scale Image from the Image menu

2. In the pop-up window, choose a percentage value greater than 100% to enlarge your image (see Figure 4-13). Alternatively, you can scale up your image by choosing from the drop-down list one of the following measurements: pixels, inches, millimeters, points, or pica. Then type into the Width area the size you need.

3. Click the adjacent chain link (see Figure 4-13). This retains the images original proportions.

4. For the method of scaling or interpolation, try Cubic or Sinc (Lanzcos3).

5. Click Scale. The image will scale up 200%.

Figure 4-14 is a photo of a computer fan before scaling up in GIMP. Figure 4-15 shows the computer fan after scaling up 200%.

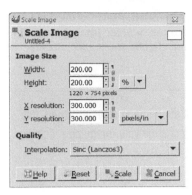

Figure 4-13. *The Scale Image window showing 200% scaling. Other scaling options are located in the drop-down list next to percent.*

Figure 4-14. *Computer fan before scaling up*

Figure 4-15. *Computer fan after scaling up 200%*

Making an Image Smaller

GIMP's Scale Image option can also scale images down in size. Choose one of the following units to scale your image:

- Pixels

- Percentage

- Inches

- Millimeters

- Points

- Pica

There is a Scale Tool in the Toolbox. However, for these exercises, as mentioned earlier, we are using the Scale Image option located in the Image menu (Image ➤ Scale Image). The Scale Image option also has an area to change the resolution of an image.

1. Go to the Scale Image option located in the Image menu, as shown in Figure 4-16.

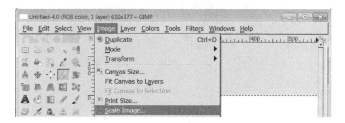

Figure 4-16. *To make an image smaller, go to Image ➤ Scale Image.*

2. In the pop-up window, choose pixel from the drop-down list near Width and Height, and type in the pixel width for your image (see Figure 4-17). Alternatively, you can scale down your image by choosing an option from the drop-down list.

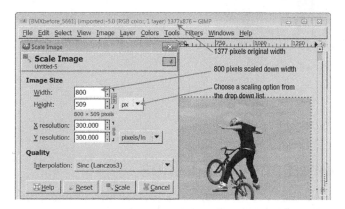

Figure 4-17. *To scale down the image for a web site, pixels were chosen from the drop-down list.*

3. Click the chain link located next to Width and Height; this retains the correct proportions.

4. For the method of scaling or interpolation, try Cubic or Sinc (Lanzcos3).

5. Click Scale.

See Figures 4-18 and 4-19 for a before and after scaling example.

Figure 4-18. *BMXer photo before scaling down for web site use*

Figure 4-19. *The BMXer photo scaled down to 800 pixels wide*

Fixing Perspective: Leaning Buildings

GIMP has a powerful Perspective Tool. Use the Perspective Tool to correct a photo that has leaning buildings or towers or power poles etc. (see Figures 4-20 and 4-21)

Figure 4-20. *Leaning building before using GIMP's Perspective Tool*

Figure 4-21. *The same building after using the Perspective tool. Note that a small amount of the image has been cropped.*

The following exercise shows you how to straighten an image. Once you have completed the exercise, feel free try different options in the tool.

To straighten a leaning building, follow these steps:

1. Open your image in GIMP.

2. Click on the Perspective Tool located in the Toolbox (see Figure 4-22).

3. Below the Toolbox are the Tool Options for the Perspective Tool. Select the following Tool Options (see Figure 4-22):

- Direction: Corrective (Backward)

- Interpolation: Sinc (Lanczos3) - optional

- Clipping: Crop to result

- Preview: Image

- Guides: Number of lines, try 15

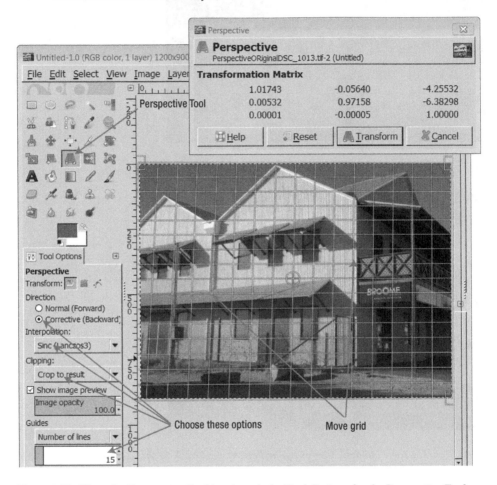

Figure 4-22. *When the Perspective Tool is selected, the Tool Options for the Perspective Tool are available.*

4. Click on the image to activate the Perspective Tool. A grid will appear over the image and a pop-up dialog box will appear, as shown in Figure 4-22. Move the dialog box off the image so you can see what you are doing.

5. Move the grid with your mouse, so that it lines up with vertical lines on your image.

6. Click on Transform in the dialog box. If you're not happy with the result, you can go back a step in your Undo History or click Control+Z on your keyboard.

7. Your image will have a hatched border down two sides (see Figure 4-23). This is because "Crop to result" was selected to give your image clean, straight edges.

8. To remove this blank space, go to Image ➤ Autocrop Image (Figure 4-24).

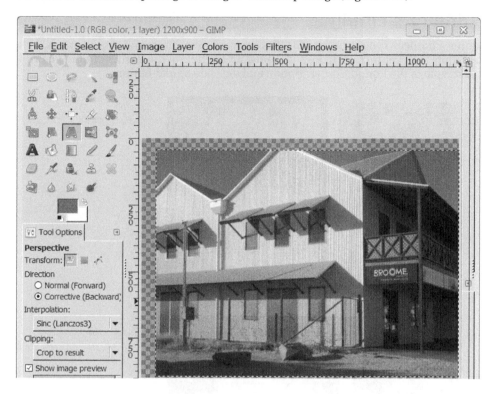

Figure 4-23. *After the Transform, and with "Crop to result" selected, the image has a blank or transparent edge on two sides.*

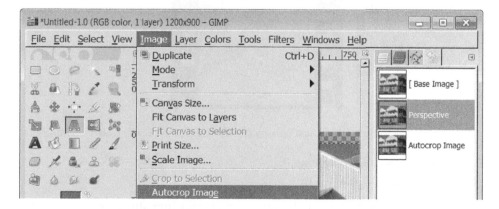

Figure 4-24. *To remove the hatched border go to Image ➤ Autocrop Image.*

81

9. To save your image, go to File ➤ Export and save your image as a JPG or TIF. Or click File ➤ Save to save your image in GIMP's native file format which is XCF.

Framing an Image

Adding a border to your image in GIMP is easy. Framing effects and other options are located in the Filters ➤ Decor menu. Figure 4-25 shows an example of the Border option. Figure 4-26 shows an example of the Round Corners option and the Slide border option.

Figure 4-25. *The image on the left has no border; the image on the right has a border.*

Figure 4-26. *The image on left has round corners and the image on right has GIMP's Slide option.*

To add a frame, follow these steps:

1. Open an image in GIMP.

2. Go to Filters ➤ Decor and choose a border type from the menu (see Figure 4-27).

3. To save your image, go to File ➤ Export to save your image if it is a JPG or TIF. Or click File ➤ Save to save your image in GIMP's native file format of XCF.

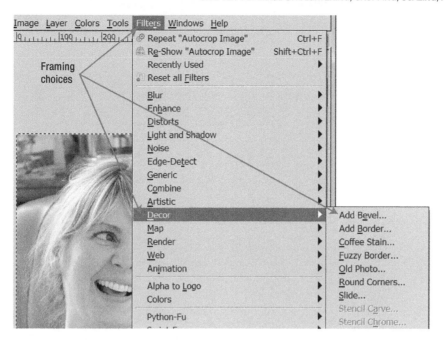

Figure 4-27. *There are several framing effects available in the Filters ➤ Decor menu.*

We will be looking at more filters throughout the book.

Summary

This chapter covers everything to do with the perimeter of your image. We showed you how to add a frame or border to your image and how to crop and resize an image. We also showed you how to straighten an image and correct perspective distortion. In the next chapter, you will learn how to fix problems in images.

CHAPTER 5

■ ■ ■

Fixing Problems in Images

In This Chapter

- How to assess problems in images

- How to fix a range of problems in images

As a beginner, you may want to improve a digital image but are unsure of the best way to do this with GIMP. Maybe you have some scanned photos or digital images that need a little improvement. This chapter will show you where to find the tools to reduce or eliminate a problem in your image.

To help you assess problems with your images, this chapter has a gallery of photos with common problems and their solutions. Some of the images are recent and some of the images are over a hundred years old. They include images that are too bright, too dark, are lacking in color, have too much color, or are flat and dull. The gallery also has examples of sharpening, removing spots, removing red eye, and whitening teeth.

Assessing Images

You don't need to be an expert to assess the faulty areas of a photo. It just takes common sense. Open the image you would like to improve in GIMP and take a good look at the image. (See Chapter 2 if you need help with opening an image). Ask yourself the following questions:

- Is the image too bright?

- Is the image too dark?

- Is the image dull or lacking in contrast?

- Is the image lacking sharpness; in other words, is it out of focus or unclear?

Look through the pictures in the gallery below and see if you can spot a similar problem to your problem.

Image Assessment Gallery

The gallery in Table 5-1 shows images with problems. There is often more than one way to improve an image. GIMP is packed full of options. You can take easy steps or steps that are more complex. Most of the more complex tools give you a greater degree of control. The easy options are listed first. Most of these tasks are fun to do, particularly when you make real improvements to favorite images.

The quality of your result depends on the quality of your original image.

Table 5-1. *The Before and After Gallery*

Before (Image Problem)	After (GIMP Solution)	GIMP Location
Is the image too bright?	Brightness-Contrast	Menu Colors ➤ Brightness-Contrast Or Colors ➤ Levels (Levels gives more control than Brightness-Contrast)
Is the image too dark?	Levels	Menu Colors ➤ Levels
Antique, old, dark photo	Curves	Menu Colors ➤ Curves (Curves gives more control than Brightness-Contrast)
Image lacks contrast	Brightness-Contrast	Menu Colors ➤ Brightness –Contrast Or Colors ➤ Levels Or Colors ➤ Curves

Before (Image Problem)	After (GIMP Solution)	GIMP Location
Image lacks contrast	Curves	Menu Colors ➤ Curves
Image colors are too rich	Hue-Saturation	Menu Colors ➤ Hue Saturation
Unnatural color cast or color balance	Hue- Saturation	Menu Colors ➤ Hue Saturation
Noise in a photo	NL Filter	Menu Filters ➤ Enhance ➤ NL Filter
Image needs sharpening	Unsharp-Mask	Menu Filters ➤ Enhance ➤ Unsharp-Mask

continued

Before (Image Problem)	After (GIMP Solution)	GIMP Location
Red eyes	Red Eye Reduction	Menu
		Filters ➤ Enhance ➤ Red Eye
Whitening teeth	Dodge Brush	Toolbox
		Dodge Tool (Brush)
Lightening the football	Dodge Brush	Toolbox
		Dodge Tool (Brush)
Darkening the background	Burn Brush	Toolbox
		Burn Tool (Brush)
Removing spots	Smudge Brush	Toolbox
		Smudge Tool (Brush)
Removing spots	Healing Brush	Toolbox
		Healing Brush and Colors ➤ Curves
		Better option than the Smudge Tool.

Assessing Brightness and Darkness

Take a good look at a photo you wish to work on. To help you assess the faults in your images, we will explore some terms a little further.

Too Bright (Overexposed)

In Figure 5-1, the top photo has blown highlights and pale colors; it lacks contrast. The bottom image has been edited in GIMP. It is not a perfect repair. However, the process improves a 30-year-old image.

Figure 5-1. *Notice the blown highlights in the taller boy's shirt and on the grandfather's head in the top photo; it also lacks contrast. The bottom photo is the result of corrections made in GIMP.*

Too Dark (Underexposed)

The top image in Figure 5-2 is very dark. This is an example of an underexposed image. The bottom image is the same image after editing in GIMP.

Figure 5-2. *The top image was taken with a two-year-old digital camera; it was underexposed, resulting in a very dark image. The bottom photo is the same image after editing in GIMP.*

Image Too Dull (Lacking Contrast)

An image that is dull has poor contrast and lacks snap. A dull image usually lacks black. Look at the top image in Figure 5-3 below; there are dark tones but not a deep black. Similarly, although the photo contains some white in the clouds and in the caps on two of the tourists, that white is dull.

Figure 5-3. *The top image is flat; it lacks contrast. The bottom image has been edited in GIMP.*

Assessing Your Editing

After assessing the problems in your image, the next step is to start editing the image in GIMP. When working on your images, zoom to 100% (to zoom to 100%, type 1 on your keyboard). Chapter 2 has more information on zooming. There are times when you may want to zoom in more than 100%, particularly when you are working on fine details.

Before you save or export your image, you need to decide where the image will go. Is it to be a printed image or will the image be shown on a digital frame, a web page, or e-mailed to friends? The wrong choice of resolution and image file type might waste a lot of your editing time. Go to Chapter 3 if you need help in choosing the best resolution and file type for your image.

Editing Checklist

As you start to correct your image, check that you can see details in the highlights, midtones, and shadows. If you overcorrect, some parts of the image may look great but this change may adversely affect other parts of the image. For example, you may be able to bring a lot of detail back into a washed out area but lose definition in darker areas of an image. If this does happen to you, do not despair, these problems can sometimes occur when you edit the whole image. In Chapter 6, we show you how to adjust part of an image, using selections, while leaving other parts untouched.

Areas of GIMP Used in This Chapter

Most of the activity in this chapter takes places in the Colors menu. Figure 5-4 shows you where the Brightness-Contrast, Levels, and Curves options are located in the Colors menu.

When we give a direction such as go to Colors ➤ Brightness-Contrast, it means go to the Colors menu as seen in Figure 5-4 and click the word "Colors" to open the menu. Scroll down the menu list until you come to Brightness-Contrast. Click Brightness-Contrast to open a small Brightness Contrast dialog window.

Undoing an Edit with Undo History

When editing, you can change your mind using GIMP's Undo History. See Figure 5-4. Each mouse click results in a temporary thumbnail image in Undo History. To move back, click on a thumbnail image in your Undo History.

The Undo History is not saved when you export or save your image. See Chapter 10 to increase the number of undo steps.

The keyboard shortcut to undo one action is Control+Z or Command+Z for Mac.

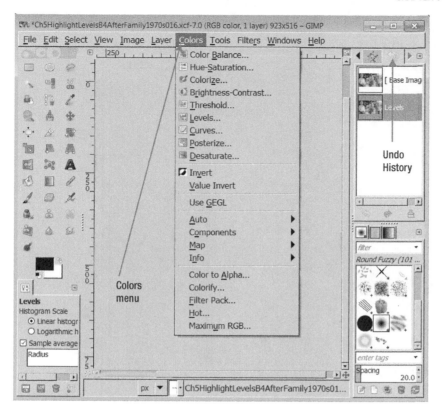

Figure 5-4. *The Colors menu and the Undo History area. Some menu items will be grayed out if you look at them without having an image open in GIMP.*

Correcting with Brightness (Contrast)

Brightness-Contrast is a convenient tool for beginners. It consists of two easy-to-use sliders. (GIMP has two other solutions that are more powerful: Levels and Curves.)

Keep in mind the aim as you edit is to increase the contrast without losing fine details in the photo.

1. Open your image in GIMP.

2. Go to the Colors menu, scroll down and click on Brightness Contrast (see Figure 5-5). This screenshot shows the GIMP workspace in single-window mode with three images open. To access single-window mode, go to Windows ➤ Single-Window Mode. If you have more than one version of an image open, you can click from one image to the other to compare your edits.

93

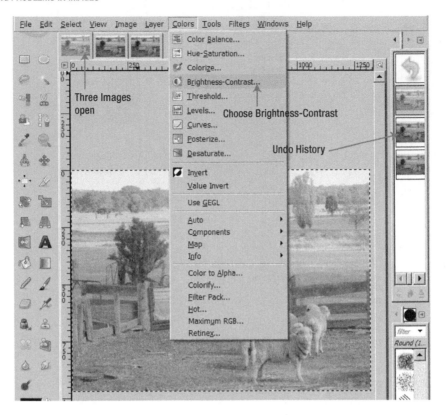

Figure 5-5. *Brightness-Contrast is located in the Colors menu. Notice the Undo History on the right. You can click back to undo an edit. You can also have more than one image open and click on an image to compare it.*

3. Figure 5-6 shows the Adjust Brightness and Contrast dialog window. This is how the Adjust dialog looks before any adjustments.

Figure 5-6. *The Adjust Brightness and Contrast dialog window with no adjustments. Ticking the Preview box will allow you to see the changes to the image on your screen.*

4. Tick the Preview box in the Adjust Brightness and Contrast window. This will allow you to see the changes you make to your photo when you move the sliders.

5. For an image that is too bright, try moving the Brightness slider to the left. If you have an image that is too dark, move the Brightness slider to the right. If your image lacks contrast, try moving the Brightness slider to the left and the Contrast slider to the right (see Figure 5-7).

Figure 5-7. *Example adjustments for an image lacking in contrast.*

6. To check your adjustments, click Preview on an off. If you are unhappy with the adjustments, click the Reset button to reset the sliders back to zero.

7. When you are happy with your adjustments, click OK. Then click File ➤ Save or File ➤ Export to make the change permanent (see Chapter 3 for help saving or exporting an image). See Figure 5-8 for a before and after view using Brightness-Contrast.

Figure 5-8. The top photo before editing; the bottom photo after using Brightness-Contrast.

Improving Tones in Images with Levels

In addition to Brightness-Contrast, Levels and Curves are two more options available in GIMP for adjusting tones in an image. They are useful for repairing images that are overexposed (too light), underexposed (too dark), and lacking in contrast (too dull). This section looks at using Levels to improve your image.

The Levels option is relatively new. There are many ways to use Levels, some techniques are quite complex. This section looks at a couple of easy ways of improving photos with Levels. The Levels option is located at Colors ➤ Levels (see Figure 5-9).

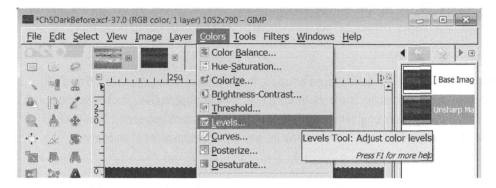

Figure 5-9. *To get to Levels, click Colors, scroll down, and click on Levels*

Look at the Levels pop-up dialog window in Figure 5-10. The graph you see is called a histogram. The histogram gives visual measurements of the tones in your image. At the left end of the histogram are the dark-to-black tones and at the right end of the histogram are the lighter-to-white tones. The height of the graph indicates the amount of a tone in the image.

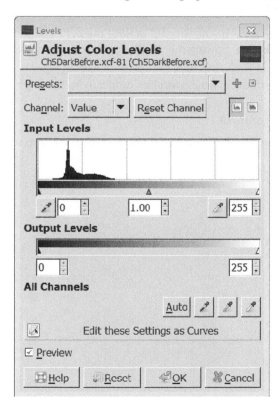

Figure 5-10. *The Levels pop-up window or dialog. This histogram is showing most information at the dark end of the spectrum.*

When working with Levels, the focus for beginners is on the Input Levels. A lot is possible using the Input Levels area. Output Levels is not intuitive and perhaps not for beginners.

■ **Note** Channels: In GIMP, digital color images are made from a mixture of red, green and blue (RGB). Color is stored in red, green and blue channels. In some GIMP's editing options such as Levels and Curves, you can edit individual channels for greater control. Value refers to the combined output from the RGB channels. The Alpha channel (when present) controls the amount of transparency in an image.

The Channel Area is set to Value by default, this is a mix of the red, green and blue channels. However, once you are confident using Levels, you can experiment by opening the drop-down Channel list and try altering the red, blue, or green channels separately. Every image is different so this is an area where playing around with individual channels may bring something useful for your image.

Improving a Low Contrast Image with Levels

1. Open your image in GIMP and access Levels in the menu system by going to Colors ➤ Levels (see Figure 5-9). This screenshot is also showing the GIMP workspace in single-window mode.

2. Here is a reminder in case you are not working in single-window mode: to access it, go to Windows ➤ Single-Window Mode.

3. The Levels pop-up dialog is shown in Figure 5-10.

4. Make sure the Preview box is ticked in the Levels dialog box so you can see the effects as soon as you make adjustments.

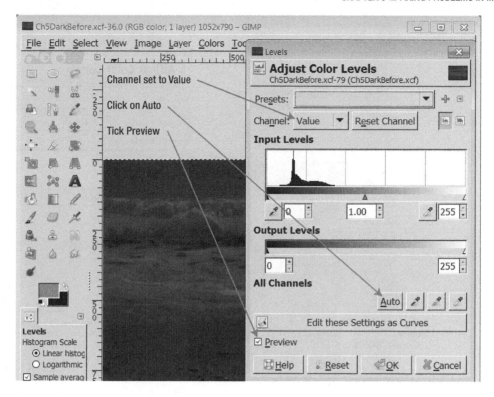

Figure 5-11. *The Levels dialog window. Make sure Preview is checked so you can see the changes on your screen.*

5. In the Levels window, check that Channel is set to Value (see Figure 5-11).

6. Then click Auto (see Figure 5-11).

7. Now try moving the middle slider, as shown in Figure 5-12. You can judge how far you need to move the slider by looking at its effect on the image. Click the Reset button if you are unhappy with your choices.

8. When you are pleased with the image, click OK.

9. Then save or export your image.

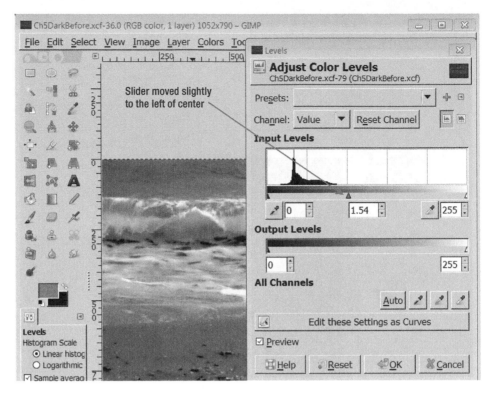

Figure 5-12. *After Auto was applied to the image, the middle slider was moved until the image looked good.*

■ **Tip** Black and White Images in GIMP

If you are working with black and white images, don't be put off by the Colors menu. The Colors section works just well with black and white images because it works on tones. Tones exist in color and black and white images.

Improving an Old Photo with Levels

The image in Figure 5-13 was found in an old box of papers. It had darkened over the years and seemed beyond repair. After scanning, the image was edited in GIMP. Sometimes an image is not aesthetically brilliant but is still of value to family members as a rare glimpse of a past time.

Figure 5-13. On the left is a dark, scratched image from 1915; on the right is the same image after Levels were adjusted.

Levels Disadvantage

Using Levels produces a good tonal range but sometimes there is a noticeable loss of color. Of course, this is not a concern if your image is black and white. One of GIMP's most popular and effective color tools is next: Curves.

■ **Tip** The Curves Tool is one of GIMP's most popular tools because it offers a lot of control over tones and colors. It's worth trying.

Correcting a Dull Image with Curves

Many people say Curves is their favorite tool in GIMP. It has some simple options for beginners and more complex options for the adventurous. The Curves Tool works on every tone in an image. It can make changes to the brightest part of the image as well as the dark areas. Like the Levels Tool, you can work on the whole image or work on the red, blue, and green color channels separately. People generally work on all channels together.

The S Curve

To add some contrast to a dull image, follow these steps:

1. In the top menu, go to Colors and click Curves (see Figure 5-14). The Curves dialog or window will open.

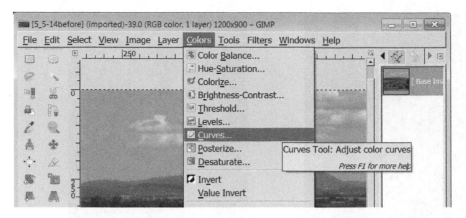

Figure 5-14. *To access Curves, go Colors, scroll down, and click Curves.*

2. In the Curves pop-up window, tick the Preview box (see Figure 5-15). This will allow you to see changes you make directly on the screen. The peaks in your histogram show you where the tones are in your image. A peak in the graph towards the left of your screen represents the dark tones; a peak in the middle is the middle or grayish tones. Peaks at the extreme right end of the graph shows the amount of highlights in an image.

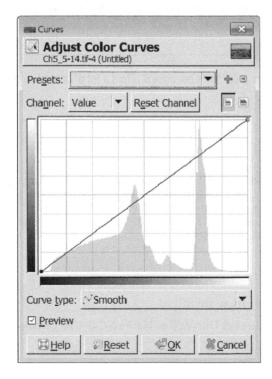

Figure 5-15. *Curves has a graph known as a histogram. The left side shows the darkest tones; the right side shows the white end of the range. Note that the Preview box is ticked.*

3. Use your mouse on the central line in the histogram to make a small S shape, as shown in Figure 5-16.

4. Click Preview on and off so you can compare your changes with the original image.

5. How small or big your S curve needs to be depends on the image. Keep checking the screen as you work to make sure you are adding the correct amount of brightness and darkness. If you start to lose details in the image, you've moved the line too far.

6. Click OK when you have improved the contrast and kept details in the highlights and shadows.

7. Save or Export your image. See Chapter 3 if you are unsure how to Save.

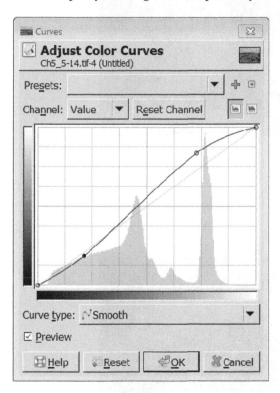

Figure 5-16. *The center line in the Curves histogram is now a gentle S shape.*

See Figure 5-17 for a before and after example using Curves.

Figure 5-17. *The top photo before editing in Curves; the bottom photo after a gentle S curve was applied.*

Figure 5-18. *A photo from 1915. In the bottom photo, the contrast has been improved by applying a small S curve in Curves.*

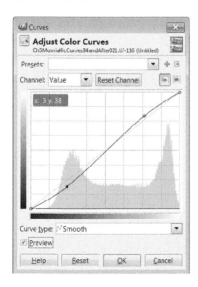

Figure 5-19. *The curve graph for the photo in Figure 5-18. Notice the very slight S curve.*

Improving Color and Tone with Curves

Extending the Histogram

There is another easy way to improve the tone and color of a photo using Curves. This method involves moving the brightest point and the darkest point towards the middle of the histogram. You will be extending the tonal range of the photo by removing tones without information in them. Try this exercise; you will see a difference in your image.

1. Go to Colors ➤ Curves. (Go back to Figure 5-14 if you are unsure.)

2. In the Curves pop-up window, click the Preview button so you can see changes you make to the graph in your image (see Figure 5-20).

3. In the Curves Histogram, move each end of the diagonal line to the start of the image information. For an example look at the lower histogram in Figure 5-20.

4. Check your changes with the original image by clicking on the Preview box.

5. Click OK when the image looks brighter and more natural.

Figure 5-20. *The top shows the image and graph before using curves to improve brightness and tonality; the bottom image is the result of applying Curves.*

Color Too Strong (Oversaturated)

The top image in Figure 5-21 is oversaturated; the red colors don't look natural. One of the easiest ways to correct oversaturation is using GIMP's Hue-Saturation.

107

Hue-Saturation

The Hue-Saturation Tool is useful for reducing the amount of color in an image. The top image in Figure 5-21 is oversaturated or has too much color.

Figure 5-21. *The lower image has been desaturated using Hue-Saturation*

Removing Strong Colors

To desaturate or reduce color that is too strong and unnatural in an image, follow these steps:

1. Open your saturated image in GIMP.

2. Go to Colors and click Hue-Saturation (see Figure 5-22).

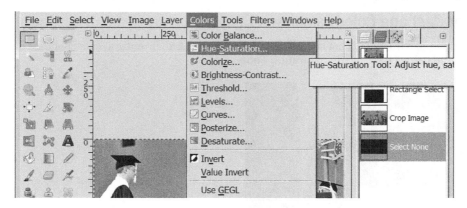

Figure 5-22. *Hue-Saturation is located under the Colors menu.*

3. The Hue-Saturation dialog window will open (see Figure 5-23).

4. Click the Preview button, to see the changes you make directly on the image.

5. Slide the Saturation slider to the left. This takes some of the color from your photo. This may be all you need to do. However, you may find that the colors then don't look natural. Try moving the Hue slider to the left and or right to correct the colors (see Figure 5-23).

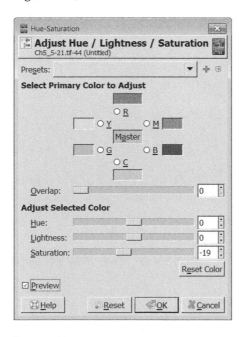

Figure 5-23. *The Saturation slider moved to -19.*

6. When the colors in your image look natural, click OK. Then Save or Export your image.

Color Cast and Color Balance

The top image in Figure 5-24 below has a red color cast. The unnatural color balance can be corrected using GIMP's Hue-Saturation Tool.

Figure 5-24. *The top image has a red color cast; the lower image was corrected using Hue-Saturation.*

Noisy Image

A noisy image is an image that has a large number of unwanted tiny colored dots scattered throughout a photo. If there is noise in a photo, it will be most noticeable in the dark areas. In Figure 5-25, the top image has noise scattered all over it.

Figure 5-25. *The top image is noisy; it has tiny unwanted colored pixels sprinkled over the image. The lower image has had the noise reduced using GIMP's NL Filter*

A noisy image can occur when you are taking photos in low light. Noise can also occur on images when you wind the sensitivity or ISO up on your digital camera. The NL Filter is a good noise reduction filter. This filter works on the whole image; in comparison, the Filters ➤ Enhance ➤ Despeckle Filter can work on a selected area of an image.

Noise Reduction NL Filter

The NL (Non Linear) Filter is useful for reducing or removing noise in an image.

1. Go to Filters ➤ Enhance ➤ NL Filter (see Figure 5-26).

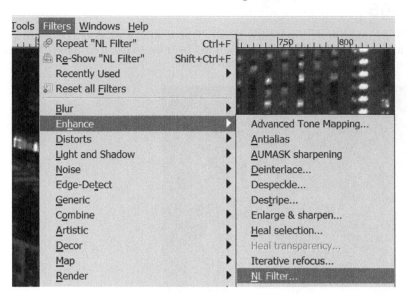

Figure 5-26. *The NL Filter helps reduce noise in images.*

2. Tick the Preview box so you can see the changes in the pop-up NL Filter box (Figure 5-27 below).

3. Choose the filter setting "Alpha trimmed mean." See Figure 5-27.With this setting, the filter looks at tiny groups of pixels and removes any pixels not like its neighbors.

4. Choose Alpha slider: .0

5. For Radius, try between .50 and 1.0. Check the effect on the dark areas of your photo in the Preview area. Adjust the radius until you see the best reduction of color noise.

6. Click Ok when you see the image has less noise. Then Export or Save your image.

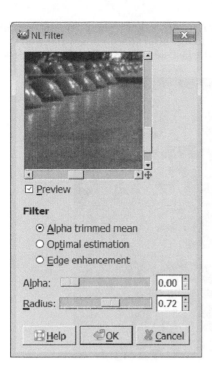

Figure 5-27. *Try using the NL Filter to reduce noise in your photos.*

If you can't see your NF filter once selected, or if it disappears, go to Filters ➤ Reshow Filter. This will bring the selected filter action box back to the top layer of your desktop.

Sharpening an Image

The aim of digital sharpening tools is to improve the sharpness of images. An image that is badly out of focus can't be repaired but an image that is slightly soft can be improved in GIMP.

If you aren't sure what sharpening can do, look at the two images in Figure 5-28. The image on the left is slightly soft compared to the image on the right, which looks clearer. The photo on the right in Figure 2-28 was sharpened in GIMP.

So when should you use a sharpening tool?

- After you resize an image, sharpening will improve the clarity of the image.

- If you have a converted RAW file, no sharpening is applied to the image in the camera. A sharpening tool will improve the image.

- If your photo is a JPG, it will have had some sharpening in the camera and may not need more sharpening.

- If an image is soft, it is worth trying a sharpening tool.

The important thing to note about sharpening an image is that it should be the last editing process carried out on the image. Any editing on the image after sharpening will lessen the effect of the sharpening. As a rule, sharpen your image as the last step in your digital editing process.

Figure 5-28. The image on the left is slightly out of focus; the image on the right has been edited with Unsharp Mask.

A very nice sharpening tool in GIMP is the very unhelpfully named Unsharp Mask Tool (Figure 5-29). It gives a lot of control and the possibility of a good outcome. Unsharp Mask is a confusing term; it is a sharpening method that originated in Germany in the 1930s. Both GIMP and Photoshop use a digital version of this process. In contrast, Sharpen, which is also a GIMP sharpening tool, provides a limited amount of sharpening control. Use Unsharp Mask for best results.

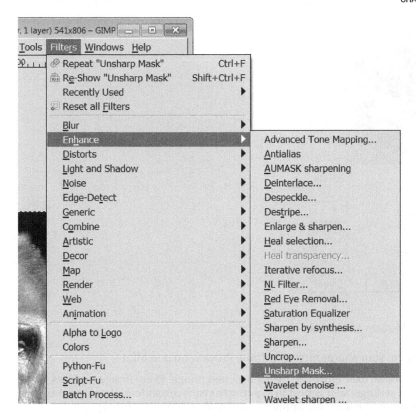

Figure 5-29. *GIMP's best sharpening method, Unsharp Mask, is located in the Filters ➤ Enhance menu.*

To Sharpen an Image with Unsharp Mask

1. Zoom in so you are at 100%. Pressing the number 1 on your keyboard will zoom your image 100%.

2. Go to Filters ➤ Enhance ➤ Unsharp Mask (Figure 5-29). Don't choose Sharpen.

3. When the pop-up dialog window opens, tick the Preview box so you can view your sharpening efforts in that window (See Figure 5-30 below).

4. Try the default setting of Radius: 5.0, Amount: .50, and Theshold: 0. This may be too harsh and overly sharp; if so, try a lower number in the Radius and Amount boxes. You can see the settings have a lower number in Figure 5-30; the default settings were too harsh for the picture taken at the zoo.

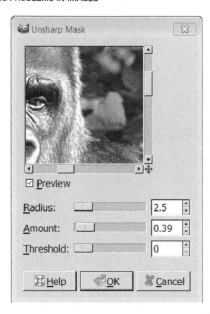

Figure 5-30. *The Unsharp Mask window*

5. Check the effect of your sharpening by turning Preview on and off.

6. See Figure 5-31 for an example of an oversharpened image. Every image requires slightly different settings, so it is best to experiment with the sliders. Usually the best sharpening effects come from the application of a small amount of sharpening.

7. When you are satisfied with the sharpening, click OK.

Figure 5-31. *The photo on the left has had a small amount of Unsharp Mask; the photo on the right has been oversharpened in Unsharp Mask.*

Removing Red Eye

Red eye is a photographic effect that accidently gives a person or animal red pupils (see Figure 5-32). This occurs when a flash is fired directly in front of the subject's face. GIMP can remove red eyes in images. The way to avoid red eye in the future is to not use a flash in front of a face. If possible, bounce the flash off a ceiling or nearby wall.

Selections

To remove red eye in GIMP, involves selecting each eye and then applying the fix. Knowing how to select parts of a photo opens up a world of editing possibilities, which we explore more fully in the next chapter.

Figure 5-32. *Top photo before Red Eye Removal; bottom photo after Red Eye Removal.*

Red Eye Removal

Removing red eye from a photo is a two-step process. First, the eyes are selected. Then the Red Eye Removal Filter is applied to the selection.

1. Zoom into your image so you are seeing it at 100% or greater. Pressing the number 1 on your keyboard will zoom your image 100%.

2. In the Toolbox, select the Ellipse tool (Figure 5-33). The tool selects an area of a picture.

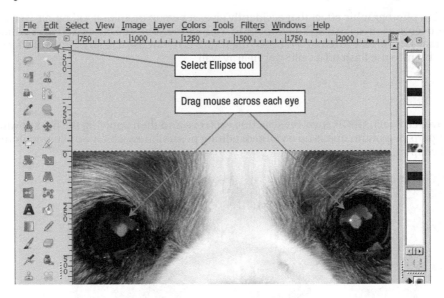

Figure 5-33. *Zoom in to see the eyes clearly, select the Ellipse Tool, and drag your mouse across an eye.*

3. With your mouse, drag an ellipse over one eye in your photo, hold the shift button, and then select the other eye. In this way you select both eyes and can work on them at the same time. If you have trouble selecting the two eyes, select one eye and complete the steps in this exercise. Then select the other eye and repeat the steps. The selection/s will allow you to apply the Red Eye Removal filter the eyes rather than to the whole image. Applying the filter without selecting the eyes would result in unusual color changes for the rest of the image.

4. To access Red Eye Removal, go to the menu Filters ➤ Enhance ➤ Red Eye Removal (Figure 5-34).

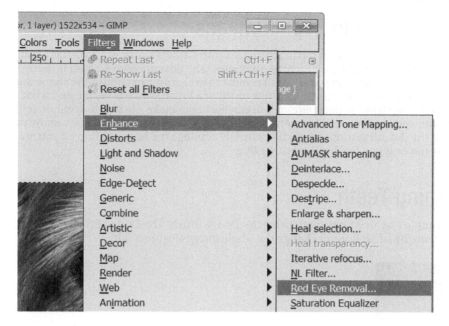

Figure 5-34. *The Red Eye Removal filter is located at Filters ➤ Enhance ➤ Red Eye Removal.*

5. In the pop-up Red Eye Removal window, tick the Preview box (Figure 5-35). This will allow you to see the changes as you move the Threshold slider. The default setting (the Threshold at 50) may work for you. If you can still see redness in the eye, increase the Threshold amount.

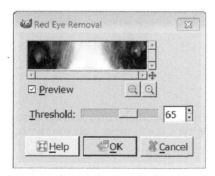

Figure 5-35. *The Red Eye Removal box*

6. Click OK.

7. To remove the selections, go to Select ➤ None or click another tool in the Toolbox.

8. Save or export your image.

Using Brushes to Repair Images

The rest of this chapter looks at repairing images with GIMP's brushes. GIMP has a range of brushes that are very useful for touching up photos. The advantage of a brush is that you are only affecting the part of the image your brush is moving over. You can choose the shape and thickness of the brush. You can choose how much of a brush stroke is visible and what percentage of the stroke is transparent. You can decide to make the brush dynamic so that the pressure and speed of your strokes behaves like a real brush. For beginners, we show you how to start using the default settings for each brush. Only change the brush options if you are not happy with the result or if you feel like experimenting.

Whitening Teeth

This is a simple way to whiten teeth using the Dodge Brush. The Dodge Brush just affects the area stroked by the Brush; it doesn't change the whole image (Figure 5-36).

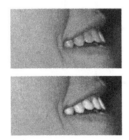

Figure 5-36. *The top photo before teeth whitening; the bottom photo after teeth whitening using the Dodge Brush*

To Whiten Teeth

To whiten teeth:

1. Open the image in GIMP.

2. Zoom in so that the teeth are very large. Try the number 4 on your keyboard to zoom in 400%. When you wish to compare at 100%, type the number 1 on your keyboard.

3. Click on the Dodge Brush in the Toolbox (Figure 5-37).

4. Located below the Toolbox are the Dodge Brush options. (When you click a tool in the Toolbox, the options below change according to the tool selected.)

5. In the Tool Options, choose Round Fuzzy Brush, Size 7.0, Dodge, Midtones, and 50% exposure.

6. In Figure 5-37, you can see the outline of the Dodge Brush over a tooth. To make your Dodge Brush smaller, choose a smaller number in the Size box in the Tool Options area (see Figure 5-37).

7. Brush once over the teeth to whiten them. If you make a mistake, use your Undo History to go back a step or two. You can also go back a step by clicking Control+Z.

8. If you find your efforts too white, change the Exposure in the Tool Options to 40% or less and try again.

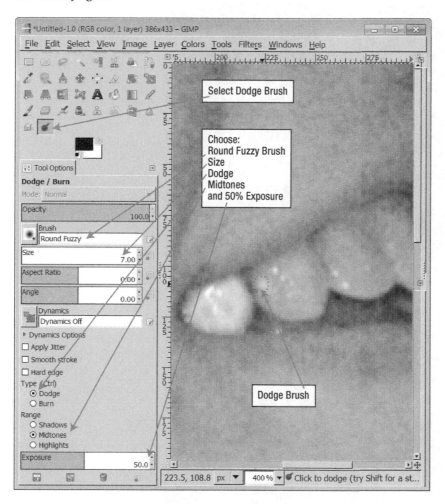

Figure 5-37. *The Dodge Brush and Dodge Options.*

Brightening Part of a Photo (Dodging)

The Dodge Brush allows you to lighten a small part of a photo without affecting the rest of the photo. The Dodge Brush is located in the Toolbox. It may be used to brighten part of a photo, such as the football in Figure 5-38, however the brush can't add in details not there in the first place.

For further information on dodging follow the example above for whitening teeth.

Figure 5-38. *The top photo is the original; the bottom photo shows dodging on the football. The football is under the arm of the kneeling player.*

Darkening or Burning part of an Image

To burn an image is to darken part of an image. You might want to darken something in the photo so that it doesn't distract the viewer from the main subject. In Figure 5-40 below, the white car was darkened with the Burn Brush.

Note that using the Burn Brush only affects the pixels the brush touches. It leaves the rest of the image unchanged. However, if you darken a washed out area too much, it will look unnatural and will not provide missing details.

1. Open your image in GIMP.

2. Click on the Dodge/Burn Brush in the Toolbox (Figure 5-39).

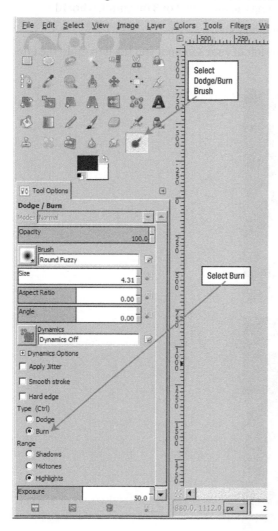

Figure 5-39. *The Dodge/Burn Brush is located in the Toolbox.*

3. In the Dodge/Burn Options box located below the Toolbox, choose Burn to darken part of your image.

4. Adjust the size of your brush using the up or down arrow in the Size area in the Tool Options. Alternatively make the brush larger by clicking] on your keyboard a few times; to make the brush smaller, click [.

5. In the Range area, choose whether you wish to work on shadows, midtones, or highlights.

6. Choose the Round Fuzzy Brush, and try the Exposure at 50%. Increasing the Exposure will increase the effect.

7. Zoom into your image by typing the number 2 or 3 on your keyboard.

8. Brush over the area you wish to darken.

9. Click on Undo History on the left of your screen if you need to undo the effect. Or type Control+Z.

Figure 5-40. *The top image is unedited. The silver car in the bottom image has been darkened with the Burn Tool.*

Unwanted Spots or Blotches

You can remove an unwanted spot in GIMP using the Smudge Brush, the Healing Brush, or the Clone Tool.

Removing Spots with the Smudge Brush

The Smudge Brush is quite easy to use but is not effective in all situations (see Figure 5-41).

Figure 5-41. *Top image has a distracting white mark high on the wall; the mark was removed in the bottom image with GIMP's Smudge Brush.*

1. Open your image in GIMP
2. Select the Smudge Brush from the Toolbox (Figure 5-42).
3. Make you brush size larger than the area you wish to smudge. In Toolbox Options located below the Toolbox, change the number in the Size area to make your brush bigger.

4. Drag the mouse over the unwanted spot with the Smudge Brush.

5. Click Control+Z on your keyboard if you wish to undo your smudge and try again.

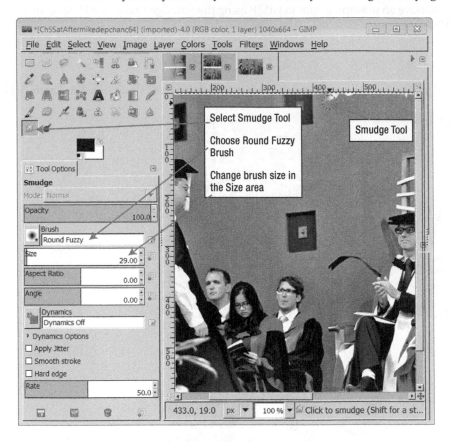

Figure 5-42. *The SmudgeTtool is located in the Toolbox. It has its own Tool Options located below the Toolbox.*

Removing Spots with the Healing Brush

Old photos can show signs of their age. They may contain unwanted spots or stains (Figure 5-43).

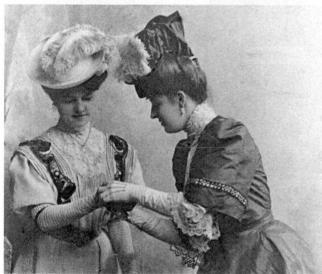

Figure 5-43. *The top image has unwanted spots and stains on the dress and throughout the 120-year-old scanned image. The image on the bottom shows the results after using the Healing Brush. The contrast was improved using Curves.*

The scanned photo in Figure 5-43 is 120 years old. It has mildew and some unwanted spots on the dress and wall in the background. Using the Healing Brush on the image helps to repair the damage of time. You could also use this technique for a color photo. The Healing Brush is useful for removing skin blemishes, spots off curtains and walls, etc.

Spot Removing with the Healing Brush

To remove spots from your image using the Healing Brush:

1. Open your spotty image.

2. Zoom into your image 150% or more. One way of zooming is to use the drop down selector shown in Figure 5-44.

3. Select the Healing Brush from the Toolbox (Figure 5-44).

Figure 5-44. *Zoom in to 100 - 150% so you can clearly see the problem area, Control+click on an area with similar texture and color to the area you want to repair.*

4. The Healing Brush will not work until you activate it. Find an area of your image with the same texture, color, and tone as your damaged area. Control+click with your mouse to select that area as the healing source. Figure 5-44 shows the healing source for the lace blouse. A separate part of the blouse was selected to remove the spot from the pleated area of the blouse.

5. Move your mouse over the unwanted spot to remove the spot and replace it with the characteristics of the source area.

6. When you are happy with your efforts, Save or Export your image.

Making Brushes Dynamic

If you want to get slightly more adventurous, you can make your brushes sensitive to pressure and speed. This option works for all brushes. In the Tool Options for your brush, click on the icon next to Dynamics and choose Basic Dynamics (Figure 5-45).

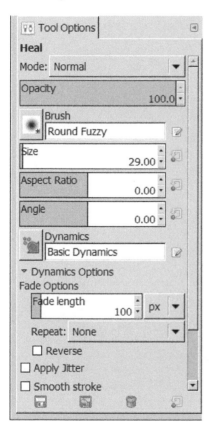

Figure 5-45. *To make a brush dynamic, click on the icon next to Dynamics and choose Basic Dynamics.*

Summary

Fixing problems in images can be rewarding and fun. The image gallery is there to help you identify common problems with images. The rest of the chapter showed you how to improve your images. The techniques in the first part of the chapter changed the whole image while the digital brushes shown later in the chapter only affect the areas touched by the brush. If you enjoyed working with brushes, making them dynamic gives you a lot of control.

The next chapter takes a leap into the world of digital creativity. It shows you more ways to select part of an image to perform a task. You can also be creative by adding photos together in layers.

■ ■ ■

CHAPTER 6

Digital Imaging Projects

In This Chapter

- Adding text to images
- Adding multiple images using layers
- Working on part of an image
- Cloning or copying parts of an image
- Applying GIMP's filters to change the look of your images

The exercises in this chapter will greatly increase your digital editing skills and expand your creative options. You can create images that in the past needed expensive professional equipment. You will learn to use layers to combine two or more images together. You will discover how to select and work on a part of an image using selections. You will see how to copy or clone parts of an image. Finally, we introduce you to GIMP's filters. Filters can radically change the way your image looks.

How Difficult Is This Chapter?

If you have completed some of the earlier exercises in this book, you should have no problems learning about selections and layers. Selections use tools from the Toolbox and Layers makes use of some menu items and GIMP's right hand panel.

The filters at the end of the chapter are easy to use. You open an image, select a filter from the Filter menu, and click OK. Some filters contain additional options that you can try out. The main danger with filters for beginners is the tendency to use them all the time.

Before and After Gallery

The gallery in this chapter has before and after photos to demonstrate the changes you can make to your images using the methods in this chapter. Look through the gallery and choose a few techniques to try on your digital projects. One of the most enjoyable parts of digital image editing is that you can try out ideas without destroying the original.

The Digital Project Gallery

Table 6-1 shows the projects covered in this chapter, featuring the before and after photos as well as the GIMP location for the tools. Each task is explained in detail in this chapter.

Table 6-1. *The Before and After Gallery*

Task	Solution	GIMP Location
Adding text to an image	Text over image	Toolbox
		Text Tool
Web banner	Transparent banner	Toolbox
		Text Tool
Combining images	Layers	Menu
		Layers
Change background	Selecting part of an image	Toolbox
		Selection Tools
		and Quick Mask
Change shape of objects	Cage Transform Tool	Toolbox
		Cage Transform Tool

Task	Solution	GIMP Location
Removing object	Removed red scarf	Toolbox Clone Tool
Color to black-and-white	Grayscale	Menu Image ➤ Mode ➤ Grayscale Or Colors ➤ Hue Saturation Or Colors ➤ Desaturate
Color to sepia	Old Photo filter	Menu Filters ➤ Décor ➤ Old Photo
Before filter	After iWarp filter	Menu Filters ➤ iWarp
Make photo look like a painting	Use a filter then add a layer to draw on	Menu Filters ➤ Artistic ➤ Oilify

133

Adding Text to an Image

It is possible to add text to any image you open in GIMP. Figure 6-1 is an image of an ant's nest with the word Enter typed next to it.

Figure 6-1. *The word Enter was added to the photo using the Text Tool.*

To add text to an image:

1. Open an image in GIMP.

2. Select the Text Tool in the Toolbox. See Figure 6-2 below.

3. Click on the area of the image where you want to put the text. A dialog box will appear.

4. Choose the color and size of the text in the text dialog box located below your Toolbox.

5. Type the text in the box (see Figure 6-2).

6. If you can't see what you typed, check to see if the text is very small or if the color of the text is the same color as the background.

Change the Color of the Text

To change the color of the text, highlight the text. In the text box options, select a color (see Figure 6-2).

Change the Size of the Text

Change the size of the text by dragging your mouse over the text and selecting a size from the Text Tool options.

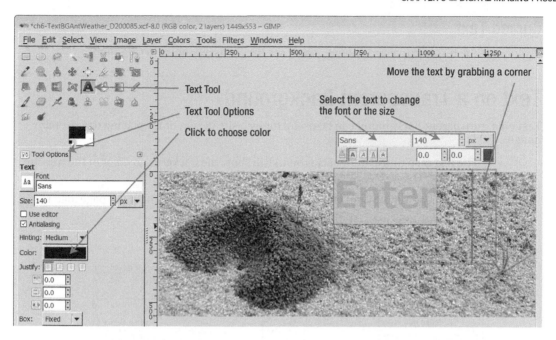

Figure 6-2. *When you click the Text Tool, a text box appears over your image. Grab a corner to move the box to the correct position, then type your text. Highlight the text if you want to make changes*

Change the Font

Change the font face by choosing a font from the text box options.

Move Text

To move the text, make sure the text is selected. Select the Move Tool in the Toolbox, click the text, and move it into position.

Deselect Text

To deselect the Text Tool, select another tool in the Toolbox.

Effects on Text

Effects or filters can be applied to text.

A popular filter for text is the Beville Filter found at Filters➤ Artistic➤ Bevel. Select your text and then apply the filter. Another filter useful for text is the Drop Shadow Filter is located at Filters➤ Light and Shadow➤ Drop Shadow....

Once an effect is applied to the text, the text can't be edited.

Curved Text

If you want the text to curve and change shape, see the paths examples in Chapter 9.

Text on a Transparent Background

Text on a transparent background can be useful for web site design or for placing text over any image.

- The text on a transparent background will show the background color of the website or image. The text will blend into the look of the web site.

- The transparent text can be a small PNG or GIF file; this will help the page load faster.

To make text on a transparent background:

1. Go to File ➤ New (see Figure 6-3).

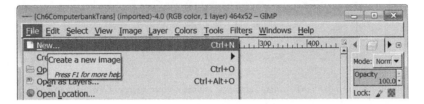

Figure 6-3. *Create a new image by going to File ➤ New.*

2. In the pop-up Create New Image window, click Advanced Options (see Figure 6-4).

3. In Advanced Options, click Transparency (see Figure 6-4).

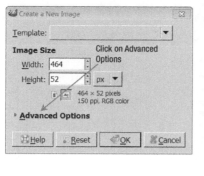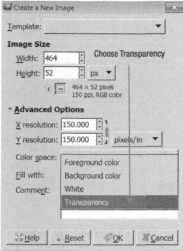

Figure 6-4. *To create a new image with a transparent background, open Advanced Options and choose Transparency.*

4. Click on the Text Tool in the Toolbox (look back at Figure 6-2 if you are unsure).

5. Click your mouse inside the blank image

6. Type your text. You will be typing over a checkered background. This checkered background lets your know your image background is transparent. (See Figure 6-5).

Computerbank

Figure 6-5. *The word Computerbank is over a transparent background.*

7. To crop the banner to fit your text, go to Image ➤ Autocrop Image (see Figures 6-6 and 6-7).

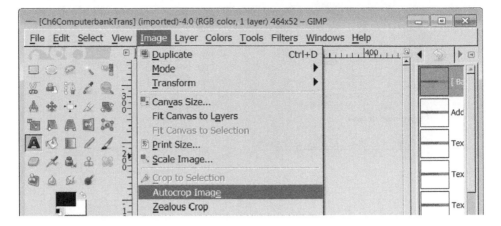

Figure 6-6. *The web banner is cropped to size by going to Image ➤ Autocrop Image.*

Computerbank

Figure 6-7. *The cropped web banner*

8. Go to File ➤ Export to save your image. To retain the transparency, you must export the image as a GIF or PNG. Figure 6-8 shows the text placed over a light blue background. Note that JPG images can't be saved with transparent areas.

Computerbank

Figure 6-8. *The transparent banner over a colored background*

Layers

You can add two or more images together in GIMP using layers. Using layers opens a world of creativity for the artistically minded.

Layers are separate images stacked on top of each other to make one picture. Usually there is a background image with one or more images placed on separate layers on top of this background layer. Placing images on different layers allows you to work on each layer separately.

Adding Two or More Images Together

In the pre-digital imaging days, it was possible to add images together by cutting and pasting. When you wanted to make up an image from parts of other images, you cut out the images and then pasted the images on a sheet of paper. Using this cut-and-paste method, you could control where each part was placed, but you couldn't change the size of any part or its transparency. If you made a mistake, you had to find more copies of the images and reassemble them.

The Layers area in GIMP allows you to

- Add two or more images together using layers.

- Change the transparency of any layer.

- Edit each layer separately using GIMP's tools or filters.

- Join layers together and edit them together.

- Change the order of the layers.

- Change which layers are visible.

- Save your layers in a XCF file to work on later.

- Export the finished image as a TIF, PSD, JPG, etc.

What Sorts of Images Can Layers Produce?

The following are some examples of images made with GIMP's layers.

In Figure 6-9, there are three separate photo layers: the text (Mungo National Park), a photo of a rock carving, and a photo of sand and rock formations.

Mungo National Park

Figure 6-9. *Three separate images: the text, the carved rock, and the landscape can be put on separate layers.*

These three picture elements were put on separate layers in GIMP. In Figure 6-10, the composite image shows the modern Aboriginal rock carving with an overview of the Lake Mungo dry lake system and the text naming the area.

Figure 6-10. *In this example of a layered image, the landscape is the background image, the rock image was placed above the background layer, and the text layer was added as the top layer.*

The second example in Figure 6-11 shows two BMX riders.

Figure 6-11. *Two photos are on separate layers in this image.*

Figure 6-12. *Two separate photos of a BMX bike rider jumping off a ramp*

Creating a New Blank Layer

To add a blank layer to your open image, follow these steps:

1. In the Layer menu, click on New Layer (see Figure 6-13). By default, a layer is created the same size as your open image; it also creates the layer as a transparency.

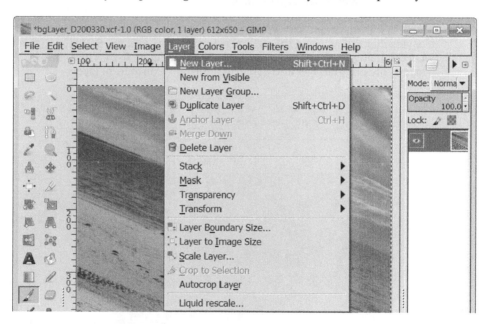

Figure 6-13. *The Layer menu*

2. The pop-up Create a New Layer dialog window gives the choice of changing the size of the layer and of choosing a foreground color, background color, white, or transparency (see Figure 6-14). (Beginners can leave the default settings and click OK).

Figure 6-14. *Create a New Layer options*

3. Here is the important part. When the new layer is created, the layer is added to the Layers dialog located on the right of your screen, see Figure 6-15. If you can't see the Layers dialog, click on the Layers icon shown in Figure 6-15. This figure also shows two layers, the original layer and above that the new transparent layer.

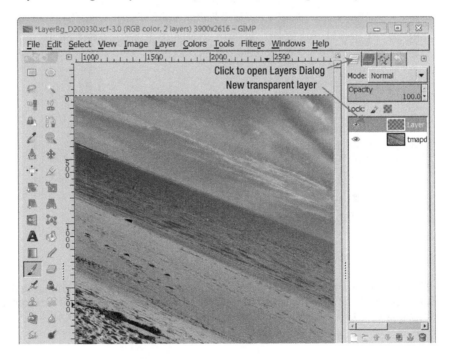

Figure 6-15. *The Layers dialog shows the new transparent layer.*

Adding a Layer with Images Open in GIMP

This example shows how to add a layer from images already open in GIMP.

1. Open two images in GIMP's single-window mode. The images appear as thumbnails photos near the top of the window, as you can see in Figure 6-16. (See Chapter 2 for further information about single-window mode.)

2. Drag the thumbnail of an image across to the second image and then keep dragging the image down on the opened image (see Figure 6-16).

Figure 6-16. Add a layer by dragging the thumbnail of an open image onto another opened image.

3. This second photo is added as a layer to the first image. Look at the Layers dialog panel on the right of the screen to see both images displayed as layers (see Figure 6-17).

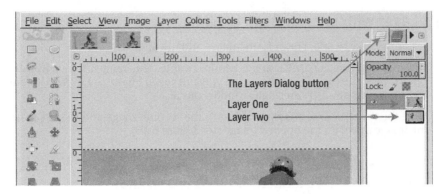

Figure 6-17. *New layers always appear at the top of the Layers dialog.*

At this point, there are two layers both with an image of a bike rider. You can use the eye icon to turn each layer on and off (see Figure 6-17). However, with both layers turned on you can only see the top layer. This is because the top layer has no transparent areas. Unless we make a transparent area on the top layer we will not be able to see the layer below.

In Figure 6-18, the eraser was used to remove part of the top layer. We can see part of the bike rider on the layer below.

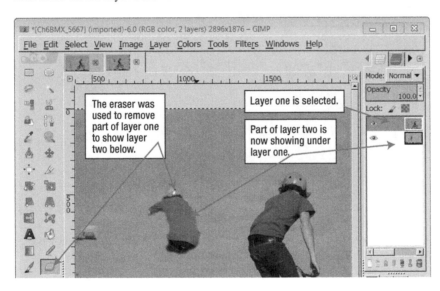

Figure 6-18. *Two layers open with part of the top layer erased*

When you click the eye icon on a layer, it turns the layer on or off (see Figure 6-19).

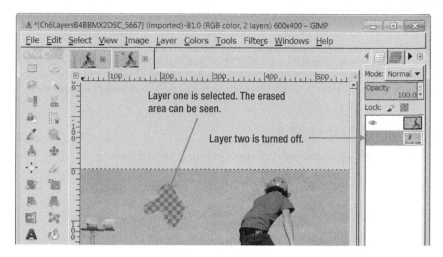

Figure 6-19. *Click the eye icon to turn a layer on or off. Layer one shows its newly erased area. Layer two is turned off.*

Opening a Layer - alternate

Another way to add a layer is go to the File menu, scroll down, and use the Open Image as Layers option.

Duplicating a Layer

In the top menu, click Layer, scroll down, and click Duplicate Layer. Look at the Layer dialog on the right side of your screen in single-window mode and you will see two identical layers.

Viewing or Hiding a Layer

The Layers panel is located on the right of your screen. Click the eye icon to turn a layer on. You can press Shift + Click on the eye icon to show the visibility of just that layer.

Click the eye icon to turn a layer off. Turning off a layer means it is not visible on the workspace. It hasn't been erased—it's just not visible.

Working on a Layer

You can only work on one layer at a time. This means the changes you make to a layer only affect that layer and not any other layers you may have.

To work on a layer, in the Layers panel on the right, click the layer you wish to work on. The highlighted layer is the active layer and is the only layer available to work on.

Linking or Grouping Layers Together

It can be useful to link related layers together to group, tone, rotate, move, or scale them. To link layers together, go to the Layers panel, select a layer, and click the blank area next to the eye icon (see Figure 6-20). A chain icon appears. Select another layer and click the area next to the eye icon to activate the link to the first selected layer. More layers can be linked by repeating this process.

Rearranging the Order of Your Layers

In the Layers dialog, drag the layer up or down to put the layers in a different order.
(See Figure 6-20.)

Deleting a Layer

In the Layers dialog, select the layer you wish to delete and click the trash can button located at the bottom of the layer (see Figure 6-20).

Changing the Transparency of a Layer

In the Layers dialog, select the layer you wish to change and then change the amount of transparency using the arrows in the Opacity area (see Figure 6-20). If you need to position two layers exactly, try reducing the transparency of the top layer to see through to the layer below.

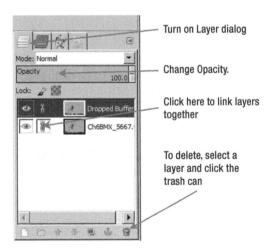

Figure 6-20. *The Layers dialog*

Erasing Part of a Layer

To erase part of a layer, in the Layer dialog, select the layer in question. Then, in the top Layer menu scroll down to Transparency ➤ Add Alpha Channel. You can now erase parts of the selected layer. The areas of the layer you erase will reveal the layer below. The checkered area shows the erased parts of the layer. A non-destructive way to erase part of a layer is by using a Layer Mask, we discuss this later in the chapter.

Merging Layers

You can merge all your layers together and remove any alpha channel by going to the Layer menu and choosing Flatten Image. Just remember this action is permanent. It is useful to do this if you are saving the image as a JPG.

Saving Layers

To save an image with its layers intact in GIMP, you can save using GIMP's XCF file format or use the Export menu to export the image as a PSD file. The PSD file will open in Photoshop or GIMP.

■ **Note** If GIMP is running slowly, it is possible to allocate more RAM for your work. Go to Edit ➤ Preferences ➤ Environment and increase the size of the file cache and the size of the Undo Memory. How much you increase the RAM depends on the RAM in your computer. If you have 2GB or more of RAM on your machine, definitely increase the RAM allocation in the Environment area to improve GIMP's performance.

Layer Masks (Non-Destructive Editing)

The Layer Mask is an advanced feature that is used to create complex layer compositions without any destructive editing. A Layer Mask offers the following benefits:

- Lets you hide or show parts of that layer.

- You control how much of a layer shows through and how much of a layer is hidden by painting on the mask.

- Painting with black on the mask makes those parts of the layer transparent. Painting with shades of gray over parts of a layer makes those parts semi-transparent. The darker the gray, the more transparent the layer; the lighter the gray, the less transparent the layer.

- Black equals full transparency; white removes any masking strokes.

- There are 256 gradations in the mask from black to white, giving a lot of control over the amount of transparency.

To add a layer mask to a layer, go to Layer ➤ Mask ➤ Add Layer Mask (see Figure 6-21).

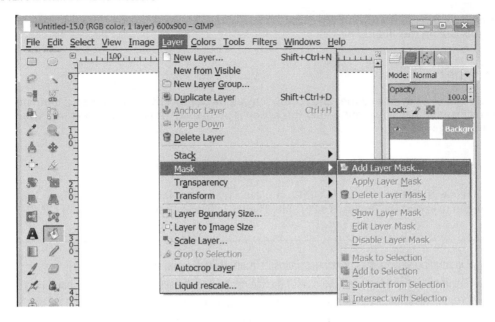

Figure 6-21. *Add a Layer Mask to hide or show part of a layer.*

When the layer mask is added to a layer, a thumbnail of the mask appears in the Layers dialog. The image in Figure 6-22 has a Layer Mask on layer one. A mask was painted on part of layer one to make it transparent. Parts of layer two below are revealed. The Layer dialog area shows the thumbnails of the layers: layer one is an image of countryside, layer two is shades of blue.

Figure 6-22. *A Layer Mask on the top layer reveals false sky on the layer below.*

In Figure 6-23 the Layer Mask has been turned off. In the Layers dialog, the Layer Mask has a red border to show it has been disabled.

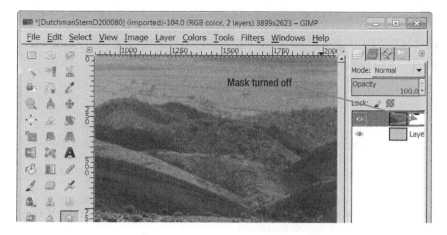

Figure 6-23. *Layer Mask turned off. The top layer of open countryside can be seen instead of the sky on layer two.*

The options for Layer Mask available at Layer ➤ Mask are shown in Figure 6-24.

Figure 6-24. *Layer Mask options are found in the top menu area at Layer ➤ Mask.*

Working on Part of an Image (Selections)

This is a very useful section for beginners.

There are times when it is necessary to work on part of an image. The ability to work on part of an image without making changes to the whole image opens a range of editing possibilities. GIMP has a number of tools available to select parts of an image. Selections are useful for the following tasks:

- Adding contrast or brightness to a part of an image.

- Adding sharpening to a part of an image.

149

- Replacing colors or textures in part of an image.

- Selecting and cutting out part of an image and adding it to another image.

- Selecting an area and changing its shape

Choosing a Selection

Sometimes parts of an image will be easy to select, like a white ball on a black background. However, if the area you want to select is very close in color and tone to the surrounding areas, the selection will take more time to complete. In cases where the colors and tones are similar, work on the contrast of the image before making the selection. (You could work on the contrast using Colors ➤ Curves .)

Figure 6-25 is an example of an easy one-click selection. One click of the Fuzzy Select Tool in the blank window space and the area was selected. The cream color was selected easily because it is in strong contrast to the dark brown window surround.

Figure 6-25. *The Fuzzy Select Tool is good for selecting areas contrasting to its surrounding areas.*

Once the window area is selected, it is possible to perform any editing task using GIMP's tools and menus. These edits will only affect the contents inside the selection.

For example, we can change the selection's color with the paintbrush from the toolbox (see Figure 6-26). The only part of the image that is active is inside the selected area. You can run a paintbrush over the entire canvas but it will only paint inside the selected area.

Figure 6-26. *The paintbrush is selected and can only paint within the selected area.*

Tools to Select Part of an Image

GIMP has the following selection tools in the Toolbox:

- **Rectangle Select** is useful for selecting squares or rectangles. Options to this selection include feather edges, rounded corners, expand from center, selection by aspect ratio, width, height, or size. (see Figure 6-27).

- **Ellipse Select** can select circular shapes within an image. Options are the same as Rectangle Select (feather edges, rounded corners, expand from center, selection by aspect ratio, width, height, or size).

- **Lasso or Free Select** selects areas by allowing clicking around the edge of the required selection, no matter what the shape. If you make a mistake selecting, unselect by clicking on another tool in the Toolbox and then select the Tool again. Options are antialiasing and feather edges.

- **Color Select** is useful if you have a plain background made up of one color. Sometimes it's easier to select a background rather than the object you want to select, which may have a range of tones and colors. Options include feather edges, select transparent areas, and threshold (which controls amount of tonal range of the color selected).

- **Fuzzy Select or Magic Wand** only selects the area the Magic Wand touches. If you click an adjoining area, the wand will select this instead. Shift click will add an area you touch. Options include feather edges, select transparent areas, and threshold (which controls the range of tones the selection).

- **Scissors Select (Intelligent Scissors)** is a great tool. Click around the edges of an object and the scissors will seek the edges. The selection must be completed by clicking on your selection starting point. If you make a mistake selecting, unselect by clicking on another tool in the Toolbox and then select the Scissors Tool again. Options include feather edges and interactive boundary. With interactive boundary selected, adjust the selected areas with your mouse. This means you can freely move the selection around.

- **Foreground Select** is used to select foreground objects. The tool has two actions; after selecting the tool, click roughly around the item you wish to select. A blue mask will appear, masking out all things excluded from the selection. Next, use your mouse to stroke across the parts of the selected area you wish to keep; each stroke helps to refine the selection. A lot of people find this tool useful.

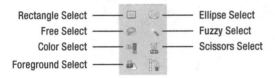

Figure 6-27. *Selection tools in the Toolbox*

Tips for Controlling Selections

Many beginners miss these very useful selection options. The Selection menu located in the top menu area is there to help you control your selections (see Figure 6-28). The Section menu contains the following options:

- **All**: You can select the whole image.

- **None**: The selection is cancelled.

- **Invert**: Rather than the inside of the selection being active, Invert makes the outside of the selection active and the inside of the selection inactive. Pressing Invert again makes the inside of the selection active again.

- **Feather**: Using Feather can make a selection look more realistic by softening the edges. Feather gives the option of feathering the edges. You control feathering by choosing the number of pixels for feathering the selection. Zoom to 100% and test with 5, 10, or 20 pixels to see what looks the most realistic.

- **Shrink**: Reduces the size of the selection.

- **Grow**: Increases the size of the selection.

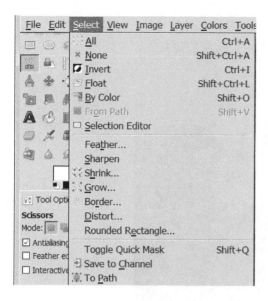

Figure 6-28. *The Select menu contains useful options to manipulate your selections.*

Selecting Tricky Areas Using Quick Mask

Selecting tricky areas usually involves selecting a part of an image that is similar in tone to its surrounding pixels. Before making any attempt at selecting, work on the contrast of the image first. You could try using Colors➤Curves.

One of the advantages of using Quick Mask is that you can see the selected areas clearly. This exercise uses the Scissors Select Tool and the Quick Mask.

1. Open your image in GIMP.

2. Zoom into the subject to be selected. Try zooming 100% by typing 1 on the keyboard or 2 for 200%. This will help you see more accurately where your selection should be.

3. Click around the subject with the Scissors Select Tool (see Figure 6-29). Close the loop by clicking at your starting point.

Figure 6-29. *Koala selected with the Scissors Select Tool*

4. Hit return. You will see an outline of the selected area.

5. To include the missed areas, select Quick Mask by clicking on the square in the lower left of the workspace (see Figure 6-30).

Figure 6-30. *The Quick Mask button is easy to miss.*

6. Use paintbrush to paint in missed areas. Zoom in to make the paint strokes easier to control. Black brush strokes add to the selection; white strokes remove parts of the selection (see Figure 6-31).

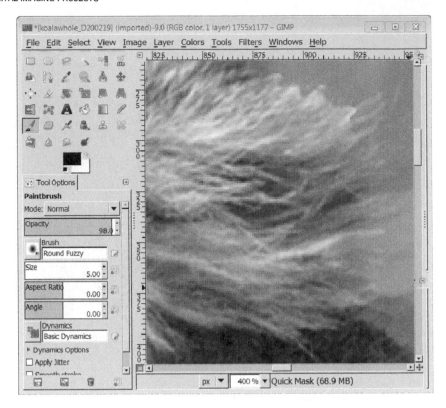

Figure 6-31. *Zoom in to paint hard to see areas.*

7. To remove the Quick Mask, click back on the Quick Mask button in the lower left of the workspace.

8. To make the selection more natural, feather your selection; try 5 pixels.

9. When the selection is complete, click on Select ➤ Invert to invert the selection. This means that any action you take affects the area outside the selection.

10. In Figure 6-32, the background was changed to black-and-white by going to Colors ➤ Desaturate and choosing Luminosity. (Alternatively, the background could be blurred by going to Filters ➤ Blur ➤ Gaussian Blur.)

11. Finally, choose Select ➤ None to remove the selection.

Figure 6-32. *After careful selection of the Koala, the background was desaturated.*

Cage Transform Tool

The Cage Transform Tool is a new feature in GIMP 2.8. This tool allows selected objects to be stretched or squashed in a natural looking way. The changes are made directly on the canvas. To transform an image:

1. Click on the Cage Transform Tool in the Toolbox, see Figure 6-33

2. Select the checkbox under the Toolbox labeled "Create or adjust the cage". See Figure 6-33. Place your selection around the object you want to stretch or squash. The more accurate your selection, the more natural looking the transformation should be.

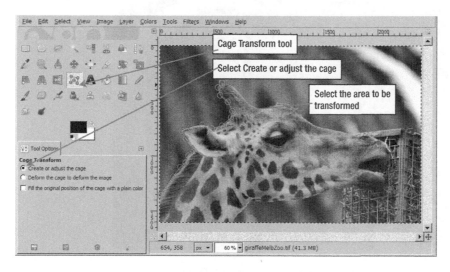

Figure 6-33. *The Cage Transform tool is selected in the Toolbox.*

3. When you have selected the object, click on the checkbox labeled "Deform the cage to deform the image". Move some of the selection points to stretch or squash part of your image. Figure 6-34 shows the Cage Transform Tool starting to work.

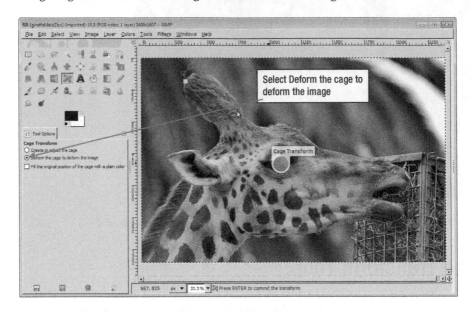

Figure 6-34. *The selection points have been moved near the horn and the Cage Transformation Tool starts stretching the horn.*

See Figure 6-35 to see the giraffe after the transformation. The extended horn looks realistic thanks to the Cage Transformation Tool.

Figure 6-35. *After the transformation process, the horn is longer.*

Cloning or Copying Parts of an Image

If you need to copy or clone part of an image, the Clone Tool located in the Toolbox is the best tool for the job. You may need to clone part of an image to repair some damage or to cover something that is distracting in a photo. You can see an example of cloning in Figure 6-36. The middle figure in the white shirt on the left image is not wearing a scarf; however, in the image on the right, he is wearing a scarf. The scarf was cloned or copied from the person next to him.

Figure 6-36. A blue and white scarf was added to the person in the middle of the picture on the right using the Clone Tool.

Cloning an Item in an Image

In Figure 6-36 a scarf is added to the person wearing a white shirt. To use the Clone Tool, follow these steps:

1. Open your image in GIMP.

2. Zoom into your image, try clicking 2 or 3 on your keyboard.

3. Choose the Clone Tool from your Toolbox. See Figure 6-37.

4. This is the most important step: the Clone Tool will not work until you activate it. Find the area of your image you wish to copy or clone. Control+Click on that spot with your mouse to select that area as the cloning source. The Clone tool will copy details from that area.

5. Now move the cloning brush to the area where you wish to add the clone information and start making some strokes. You can click Control+Z if you need to undo a step.

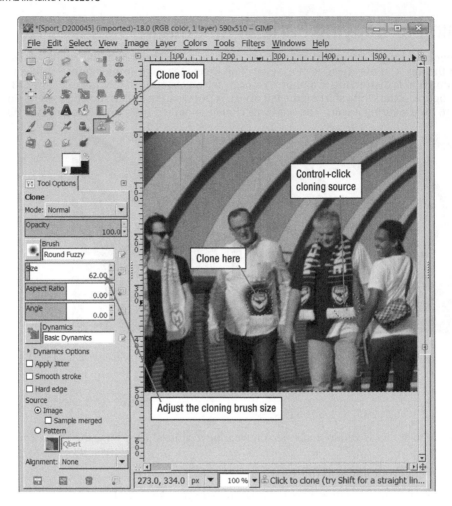

Figure 6-37. *Choose the Clone Tool from the Toolbox, Control+Click on the area you wish to clone, then brush on the area you wish to add the clone.*

6. Adjust the size of your Cloning Brush by using the slider located in the Tool Options below the Toolbox. If you can't see these options, drag on the vertical inside wall to make your Toolbox wider.

Every cloning job is different, but to give you some idea, here are the settings used for Figure 6-38:

- *Removing the Red and White Scarf in Figure 6-38*: The Clone Tool options used were Brush Round Fuzzy. Alignment was Fixed for most of the scarf removal because it was using one spot on the black jumper as the cloning source. For the skin tones. a mixture of Fixed and Aligned were used.

Figure 6-38. *The photo on the left is the original. The red and white scarf has been removed from the person in black in the photo on the right.*

Color to Black-and-White

There are a number of ways to change a color photo to a black-and-white photo in GIMP (see Figure 6-39).

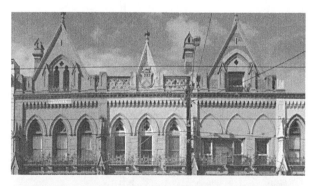

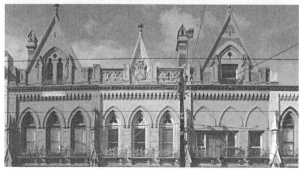

Figure 6-39. *The top image is the original color image; the bottom image has been changed to black-and-white in GIMP.*

You can change a color image to black-and-white using one of the following methods:

- Go to Image ➤ Mode ➤ Grayscale. The image is changed instantly.

- Go to Colors ➤ Hue Saturation. In the pop-up window, slide the Saturation slider all the way to the left. You can adjust the Lightness slider to your taste as well.

- Go to Colors ➤ Desaturate. In the pop-up dialog window, you have a choice of choosing Lightness, Luminosity, or Average.

- Experiment to see which black-and-white effect you prefer.

Changing the Look of Your Images with Filters

Filters change the look of your images. If you're a beginner, you may be pleased to hear that filters are easy to use. To use most filters, you simply open an image and click on a filter from the Filter menu to apply the effect.

GIMP has over 100 filters. It is not possible in the space available here to go through every filter and variation of a filter available in GIMP. Figure 6-40 shows an overview the filters types in GIMP's filter menu. Under each heading is a further list of filters for that category.

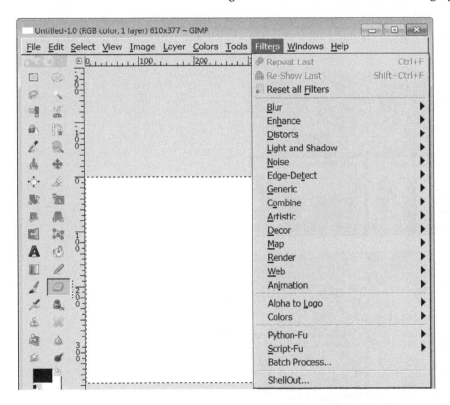

Figure 6-40. *GIMP's filters are located in the Filters menu and each listing has a submenu.*

■ **Note** Filters are very easy to use. In most cases, you simply open an image and click on a filter to apply its effects. Have fun using filters but beware! It's very easy to start using filters on nearly everything.

Old Fashioned Sepia Toning

It is easy to change a color image and give it an old fashioned look in GIMP, like the bottom image in Figure 6-41.

Figure 6-41. *The top image is the original; the bottom image has had the Old Photo filter applied to it.*

To change a color or black-and-white photo to old fashioned brown/sepia toning, open your image. In the top menu go to Filters ➤ Décor ➤ Old Photo (see Figure 6-42).

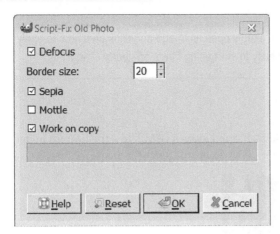

Figure 6-42. *The Old Photo Filter is located at Filters ➤ Décor ➤ Old Photo.*

The pop-up screen gives a number of options. Here's a suggestion to get you started: leave Defocus unselected, try Border 0 (unless you want a border), select Sepia, and select Work on Copy. Click OK. GIMP will make a new copy of your image and make it look old fashioned.

Warping an Image

Figure 6-43 shows an image before the IWarp filter was applied and Figure 6-44 shows the image after the iWarp filter was applied. IWarp is found at Filters ➤ Distorts ➤ IWarp.

Figure 6-43. *Photo of a gas heater*

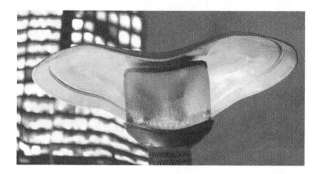

Figure 6-44. *The gas heater after the iWarp filter was applied*

Using a Filter to Convert a Photo a Background for a Drawing

Filters can be useful for artists. The Figure 6-45 shows a photo before a filter was applied. Figure 6-46 shows the photo after using the Oilify filter. Oilify is found at Filters ➤ Artistic ➤ Oilify. A new transparent layer was added to the photo and a dragonfly was drawn on it using the Paintbrush in the Toolbox, see Figures 6-46.

Figure 6-45. *Photo of waterfall used as the background for Figure 6-46*

Figure 6-46. *The photo after the Oilify Filter was applied and a new layer with a dragonfly was added*

Summary

There are countless ways to use GIMP. The gallery at the start of this chapter gives before and after views of the exercises in this chapter. Two new important steps for beginners are in this chapter, they are layers and selections. We showed you how to add images together using layers and how to select and work on part of an image using selections. We show you how to clone or copy part of an image and we gave you a taste of GIMP's many filters. Thanks to a small number of voluntary computer scientists dotted around the world, GIMP has evolved into a serious digital image-editing platform.

The next chapters look at the GIMP tools for drawing and painting.

CHAPTER 7

■ ■ ■

Setting Up a Graphics Tablet

In This Chapter

- The benefits of using a graphics tablet
- How to add a graphics tablet
- Setting up a graphics tablet

The Benefits of Using a Graphics Tablet

A graphics or digital tablet is a digital drawing tool for sketching or drawing with the aid of a computer. The tablet plugs into the computer and comes with a pen-like stylus that allows more artistic control than doing the same actions with a mouse. The stylus feels natural — not just while sketching but also while doing photo touch-ups.

When you draw on the tablet with your stylus, the drawing shows on your computer screen. The stylus is sensitive to pressure. A light stylus stroke shows on the screen as a light line and a stroke with heavier pressure shows as a darker and thicker line.

■ **Note** GIMP supports all Wacom brand tablets

How to Add a Graphics Tablet

There are three parts to setting up a graphics tablet in GIMP.

1. Check you have the correct drivers for your tablet installed on your computer.
2. Adjust access settings in the Input Device area of GIMP.
3. To get pressure sensitivity working, check that Basic Dynamics in GIMP is selected.

Installing Graphic Drivers on Your Computer

If you have been using a graphics tablet on your computer for other programs, GIMP will probably automatically detect your tablet when it opens for the first time.

If you are using your tablet for the first time on your computer, here are some general tips to get your tablet operating in GIMP. Read the section that refers to your operating system.

Windows

If you have the device drivers for your graphic tablet installed, GIMP 2.8 (and later versions) automatically detects the tablet. Because every manufacturer designs and bundles driver packages for its software differently, we do not cover how to install a driver for your tablet under Windows. If you are not sure how to install your tablet driver, look online and follow the maker's instructions.

If your tablet does not work automatically, plug in your tablet before opening GIMP. Open GIMP and then follow the instructions in the 'Setting Up Your Graphics Tablet' section below.

Mac OS X

Install your tablet's drivers in the usual way. Plug in the tablet to your USB slot. Turn your computer on. Open GIMP and follow the instructions in the 'Setting Up Your Graphics Tablet' section.

Linux

The setup is automatic for most modern Linux distributions. For example, for Ubuntu, you plug the tablet into your computer's USB slot and then turn your computer on. Open GIMP and follow the instructions in the 'Setting Up Your Graphics Tablet' section.

For other Linux distributions, it should work automatically. If GIMP is not seeing your tablet, you may need to update the drivers.

With the drivers for your tablet installed, the next step is to add the tablet to GIMP's Input Device area.

Setting Up Your Graphics Tablet

If you have your tablet drivers installed, for most people the tablet will work automatically in GIMP.

If your tablet drivers are installed and the tablet does not work automatically:

1. Plug your graphics tablet into your computer's USB slot.

2. Open GIMP.

3. Go to Edit ➤ Input Devices. See Figure 7-1.

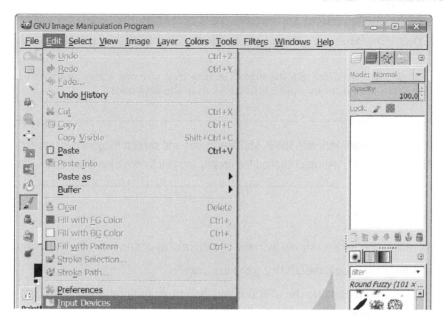

Figure 7-1. *Finding the Input Devices area in GIMP*

4. In the Input Devices screen, your graphics tablet will appear on the left hand side of the screen. Figure 7-2 has a Wacom tablet showing as an 'Input Device' in GIMP.

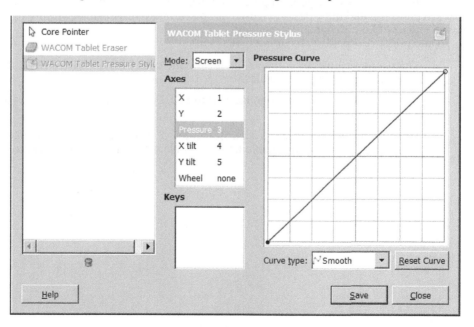

Figure 7-2. *The 'Configure Input Devices' area shows a Wacom tablet and a mouse (Core Pointer).*

5. In the Configure Input Devices area, select your graphics tablet.

6. Under the 'Mode' drop-down list for the Pressure Curve, set the device to Screen (see Figure 7-2).

7. Click Save and Close. (In the Input Devices area, you can safely ignore the Keys section. This is for mapping MIDI devices to the keyboard.)

■ **Note** Other devices also work with GIMP. MIDI keyboards and shaped triggers can map to individual keys in GIMP. For example, you could change the opacity amount by pressing a key on the MIDI keyboard.

Troubleshooting Tips

If your graphics tablet doesn't show up in the 'Configure Input Devices' screen, try these tips:

- Check that you have GIMP 2.8 or later installed.

- Plug your tablet into the USB slot and then turn your computer on.

- Open GIMP.

Adding Pressure Sensitivity to Your Tablet

Adding pressure sensitivity to your graphical pen in GIMP helps you create natural looking strokes in paintings and drawings. In Figure 7-3, you can see a brushstroke without dynamics enabled and a stroke with dynamics enabled.

To add pressure sensitivity to your tablet's pen:

1. Open a new canvas by going to File ➤ New and click OK.(See Chapter 2 for more information about opening files.)

2. Go to the Toolbox and click on the Paintbrush. Try a Paintbrush stroke on your canvas (see Figure 7-3).

3. Check your Paintbrush stroke against Figure 7-3. The top black brush stroke does not have pressure sensitivity enabled; the lower black brush stroke has pressure sensitivity enabled.

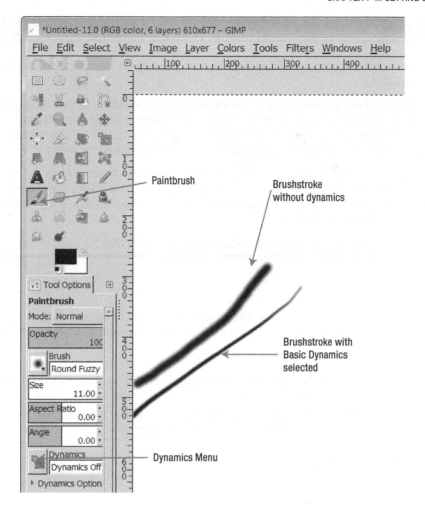

Figure 7-3. *To enable Brush Dynamics, click on the Dynamics Menu and select Basic Dynamics.*

4. To add Dynamics, in the Tool Options for the Brush, click on the icon next to Dynamics Off. In the list of choices, select Basic Dynamics. Choosing Basic Dynamics will activate pressure sensitivity for your tablet's pen.

Basic Dynamics works on the Paintbrush, Pen and the Airbrush Tools located in the Toolbox. Activating Basic Dynamics in the P:aintbrush Tool Options also sets the dynamics for the Pen and Airbrush.

If this is the first time you have used your tablet, be patient. Looking at your monitor while drawing onto the tablet feels a little strange at first. Your lines might lean at one end. With practice, this will improve. The larger the tablet space, the easier drawing will be. However, larger tablets cost more.

CANVAS RESOLUTION

If you're new to digital painting and editing digital images, you may not know about the importance of image resolution.

Before you start to draw, you need to decide on the resolution of the canvas (or new image) you are about to create. The quick and simple answer is if your artwork is for the computer and Internet only, choose a resolution of 72 dpi and export (save) the file as a JPG. If you intend to print your artwork at a printing shop, choose a resolution of 300 dpi and export your file as a TIF.

However, if you intend to work on a project over a couple of sessions, choose 300 dpi and save your file as an XCF file. XCF files are native to GIMP and store information such as layers and guides. XCF files also maintain the best quality for your work. Once your creation is completed, you can save your XCF file as a JPG or TIF.

For further information about resolution and exporting/saving, see Chapter 3.

Setting Up Your Tablet's Eraser

When the Eraser option is set up, you can turn the pen or stylus upside down and rub it on the tablet to erase unwanted parts of your work. This makes digital drawing very like using a pencil with an eraser attached to the top.

Follow these steps to set up the eraser:

1. Turn your tablet's stylus upside down so the thicker end hovers over the tablet. You should see it hover on your screen.

2. With your stylus upside down, select the Eraser Tool in the Toolbox. The Eraser Tool is near the Brush Tool and looks like an eraser (see Figure 7-4).

Figure 7-4. *The Eraser Tool is selected.*

You should now have the GIMP eraser working at the thick end of your stylus. The pointy end of the stylus is available for the brush or other tools from the Toolbox.

Summary

This chapter showed how to set up a modern graphics tablet, how to enable the pressure sensitivity option for brush strokes, and how to assign GIMP's eraser function to the top of your stylus. The next chapter covers digital drawing. However, if negotiating around GIMP is new to you, it might be a good idea to look at Chapter 2, which is all about getting to know the GIMP workspace.

■ ■ ■

Digital Art: Painting in GIMP

GIMP is not only for editing digital photographs, the tools used for photo editing are also effective for digital painting and drawing. Digital art has many facets and different styles. While you are bound by the restrictions of your camera and environment, a white canvas enforces no rules—which leaves you to paint anything that comes to your mind. As with any other creative art form, painting is a way of expressing yourself; therefore, this chapter can only tell you techniques and ways to use GIMP.

This chapter will teach you about the tools you need. If you have set up a digital tablet as described in Chapter 7, now is the time to use it.

In This Chapter

- Paint tools in GIMP

- The advantages of digital painting

- Color basics

- Using paint tools

- Layers

- Filling in the details

Paint Tools in GIMP

GIMP provides a variety of paint tools. You may have already used some of them for sketching, on photos, or for manipulating. Here we show you the purpose of the paint tools for digital painting. Most of the paint tools simulate their real-life counterparts. The pencil, for example, paints with hard edges, whereas the airbrush tool will paint with soft edges and transitions. The paint tools can be divided into three groups: the basic set, specialized paint tools, and assistive paint tools.

The basic set of paint tools includes the following:

- **Bucket Fill**: Fills larger areas of the image with the same color

- **Blend**: Creates a seamless transition from one color to another

- **Pencil**: Draws lines with hard edges

- **Paintbrush**: Draws lines with soft edges

- **Eraser**: Removes strokes or parts of the drawing

The following special paint tools also simulate their real-life counterparts:

- **Airbrush**: Draws fuzzy lines

- **Ink**: Writes lines calligraphy-style

The third set of paint tools can be used as assistive paint tools. These tools help the painter render seamless transitions or apply particular effects to the painting.

- **Clone**: Duplicates areas of the image

- **Heal**: Removes small spots in photos

- **Perspective Clone**: Duplicates areas of an image by keeping the perspective

- **Blur/Sharpen**: Sharpens or blurs edges in a painting or photo

- **Smudge**: Smears and creates seamless transitions between objects

- **Dodge/Burn**: Lightens or darkens areas in an image

Is This Chapter for Me?

In this book, we distinguish painting from drawing. This distinction is important because of the way GIMP tools are used and how a chapter is applicable to you.

Chapter 8 is most suitable if you are painting with a graphics tablet. Of course you can use a mouse to get the feel of digital painting. However for more serious digital artists using a pen with a graphics tablet will give you much greater control over your strokes.

Chapter 9 will be suitable for the digital drawer, who uses GIMP tools to emulate free strokes. If you don't own a graphics tablet, you can still create artwork—such as icons or small paintings—with GIMP.

Digital Painting: The Advantages

There are no messy brushes to clean, no paint to run or smudge and no wet canvases that could be accidentally stood on.

Digital painting in GIMP provides the following:

- A range of brushes, pencils, and airbrushes with options such as size, shape, tilt, pressure sensitivity, and opacity

- A huge range of colors to choose from

- The ability to redo or undo strokes with the press of a couple of keys

- Layers for greater artistic control: use a background layer, sketch layer, color layer, blending layer, duplicate or inverse layer, filter layer, mode layer, and so on

- The option to turn layers on or off to help the creative process

- The ability to create and save brushes and options, if needed

- The ability to copy, print, share, or publish projects to the internet

The Canvas

The canvas is a synonym for the digital image that you will paint on (see Figure 8-1). If you use GIMP with default settings, a newly created canvas will be white because the background color is white.

Later in this chapter, we will introduce layers.

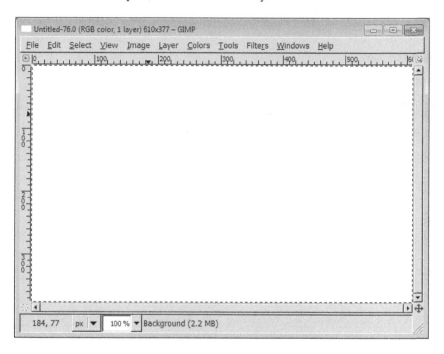

Figure 8-1. *A blank image; also known as a blank canvas*

Creating a New Canvas

Similar to the real world, where you need a canvas to paint on, you also work on a canvas in GIMP. As first described in "Creating a Blank Image" in Chapter 2, a new canvas is created by performing the following steps.

1. Open the Create New Image dialog box (see Figure 8-2).

2. If you create a painting with the intention of printing it or using a lot of detail, create the image with a higher resolution and dimensions. Use a width and height that is bigger than 1000 pixels.

3. Click the Advanced Options button to change the resolution of the painting. Use a resolution that is greater than 150 pixels per inch. Higher resolutions are important if you like to print your painting.

4. Click OK.

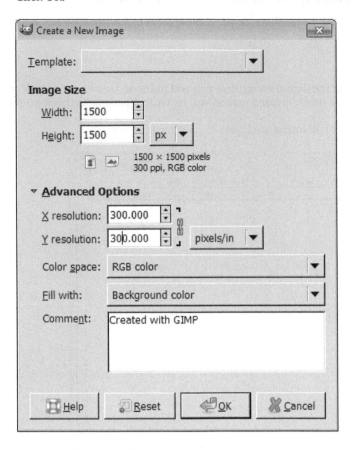

Figure 8-2. *The Create New Image dialog for creating a new canvas*

Navigation and Zooming

Depending on your style of painting, you will need quick access to tools and different zoom levels, as well as the total screen space that you have available.

How to Maximize the Work Area

GIMP allows you to focus on your canvas without losing control of your dialogs and the toolbox. If you are not using the single-window mode, you can toggle between your canvas and dialogs by using the Tab key while painting.

When painting big images, you want to use as much of the screen you can. By pressing the F11 key, you can toggle quickly between a maximized canvas and the normal canvas size. Alternatively, you can also access View ➤ Fullscreen to achieve the same effect.

Zooming and Panning the Work Area

If you paint details, you sometimes need to zoom in very quickly or alternate between different zoom levels. Zoom levels are accessible with the following numbers on your keyboard:

- 1 (100%)
- 2 (200%)
- 3 (400%)
- 4 (800%)
- 5 (1600%)

Furthermore, if you are working on details in your painting, you can pan the canvas by pressing the Space key on your keyboard or by using the second button on your pen, depending on the configuration.

Color Basics

The GIMP toolbox shows two color indicators (see Figure 8-3), representing the foreground and background colors. When creating a new image, GIMP uses the selected background as the canvas color. The foreground color will be determined by your selected paint tool.

All basic paint tools make use of the foreground and background color, indicated by the toolbox. The foreground color is set to black and the background color is set to white by default. The paper resembles the white background color and the pencil the dark pencil color, similar to the real things.

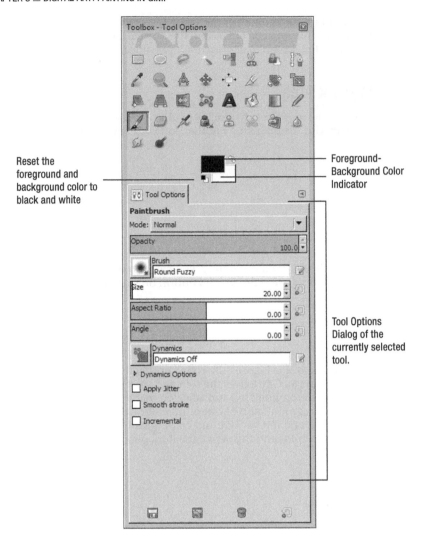

Reset the foreground and background color to black and white

Foreground-Background Color Indicator

Tool Options Dialog of the currently selected tool.

Figure 8-3. *The GIMP toolbox with the tool options dialog attached*

Choosing a New Color: The Color Dialog

A dialog box will appear if you click on the foreground or background color indicator in the toolbox (see Figure 8-4). The dialog provides different ways to choose a new color.

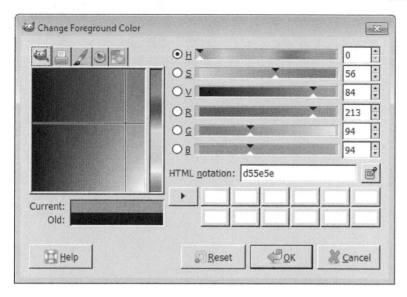

Figure 8-4. *The color dialog to select either a foreground or background color*

Colors are represented by different color models—systems that use various ways to describe colors. GIMP shows colors for different systems in the left area of the dialog box. Each color system displays all the possible colors available on your computer.

The Bucket Fill Tool

The bucket fill tool can be used for filling large areas of an image, selections, and closed areas if you are painting comics, for example. By default, the tool uses the foreground color, which is black if you just started GIMP. You can select the bucket fill tool in the toolbox or press the SHIFT+B key combination.

The tool is not only used to fill areas with the foreground or background colors; it also makes patterns that can be selected in the bucket fill tool options. You can access the tool options by double-clicking on the bucket fill tool icon in the toolbox.

Changing the Background Color

Changing the background color of the newly-created image with the bucket fill tool is easy.

1. Create a blank image. (See the "Creating a Blank Image" section in Chapter 2 if you are unsure of how to create a new image.) By default, the foreground color is set to black; the background color is set to white. The background color of your image should now be white (see Figure 8-5).

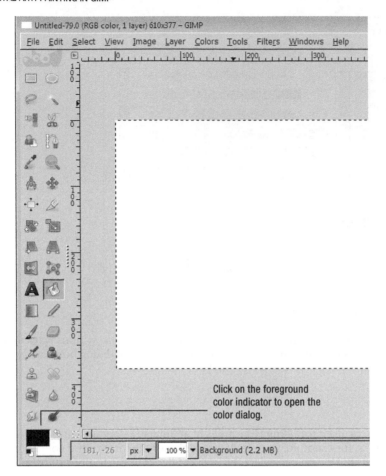

Figure 8-5. *The single-window mode setup. The color indicators open the color dialog with a mouse click.*

2. Click the foreground color indicator of the toolbox to open the color dialog (see Figure 8-6).

3. Select red as a new foreground color by clicking in the red color area. Click OK.

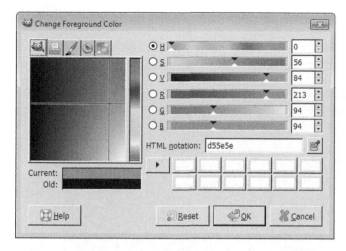

Figure 8-6. *The Change Foreground Color dialog*

4. The foreground color indicator of the toolbox should now be red (see Figure 8-7).

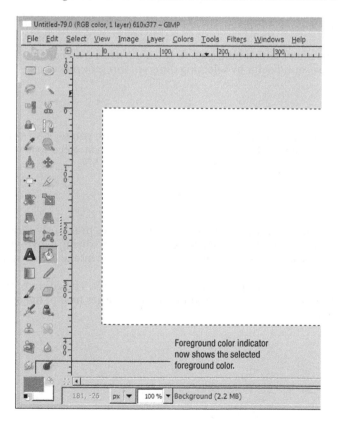

Figure 8-7. *The selected color is shown in the foreground color dialog*

5. Select the bucket fill tool in the GIMP toolbox with a mouse click (see Figure 8-8).

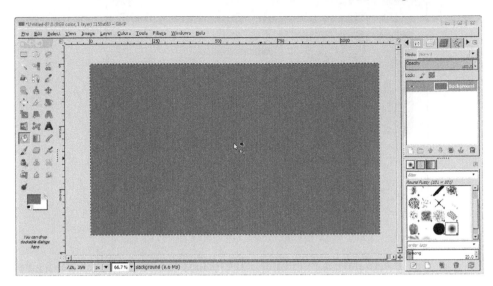

Figure 8-8. *The background color of the canvas has been filled by the bucket fill tool.*

6. Fill the canvas of the image with a mouse click. It will turn red. You can now practice and change the background color by selecting different foreground colors.

Managing Colors: Palettes

Color is a very important aspect in paintings. When painting, fairly often you need to switch between colors. GIMP provides functionality to manage the colors that you need to access again and again. Next, we will show you a variety of ways to select colors in GIMP.

The Palettes Dialog

To allow easy access, GIMP provides a way to save the colors that you've previously chosen. A range of colors can be saved in a color table, called a palette. The palette dialog allows you to browse pre-defined color tables. You access the palettes dialog from the image menu by selecting Windows ➤ Dockable Dialogs ➤ Palettes.

As shown in Figure 8-9, the Default (23) palette is selected by default. The editor of the selected palette is opened by double-clicking. The number in parentheses next to the entry indicates the number of colors.

Figure 8-9. *The palettes dialog*

The Palettes Editor

The color information in the palettes dialog is accessible by double-clicking on a selected palette, which opens the palettes editor (see Figure 8-10).

The editor works similar to the color dialog; the color you select in the editor will be set as the foreground color. The color picker tool completes the dialog, which is the central tool to add new colors to the palette.

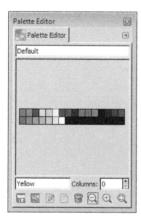

Figure 8-10. *The palettes editor allows you to manage the colors you use frequently.*

___

■ **Tip** A palette is kept independently from an image. You can always use the same palette for different paintings.

___

The Color Picker Tool

The color picker tool (see Figure 8-11) allows you to retrieve color values from your current image. This is very important during painting, as you may like to continue painting with a particular color from your image.

By default, the color picker tool sets the foreground color indicator to the color that you apply it to. The tool options allow adjusting the behavior to either, as follows:

- **Pick only**: Retrieves only the color information

- Set the foreground- or background color indicator

- **Add to palette**: Adds the selected color to the current palette

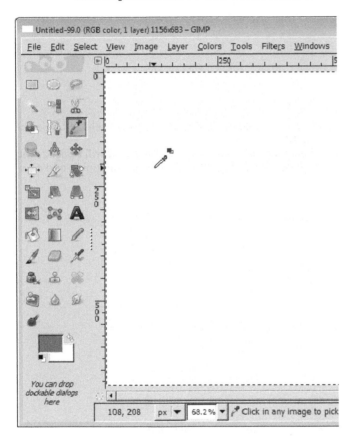

Figure 8-11. *The GIMP toolbox with the color picker tool selected. The mouse pointer changes to a pipette to reflect the selected color picker tool.*

Creating a Palette with Colors

Palettes allow easy access to the colors that you're using to paint. We'll show you how to manage your own palette.

1. Open the palettes dialog from the image menu by selecting Windows ➤ Dockable Dialogs ➤ Palettes.

2. Click the "Create a new palette" button to create a new entry in the palette dialog (see Figure 8-12).

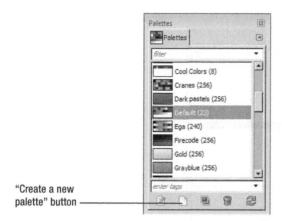

"Create a new palette" button

Figure 8-12. *Create an empty color palette with the "Create a new palette" button located on the bottom left of the dialog.*

3. The palette editor will be displayed if it is not already open. The palette dialog will have a new entry titled "Untitled" and the palette editor will show an empty, gray dialog (see Figure 8-13).

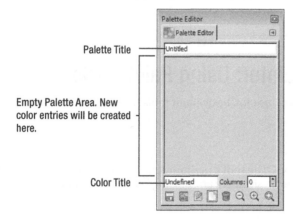

Palette Title

Empty Palette Area. New color entries will be created here.

Color Title

Figure 8-13. *A new palette entry shown in the palette editor*

4. Choose a red foreground color, as described earlier in the "Changing the Background Color" exercise.

5. Using the red foreground color, create a new palette entry by clicking on the "Create a new entry from the foreground color" button. A new color entry is created in the "Untitled" palette (see Figure 8-14). (If you click this button after GIMP started a new black color entry is created. By following this exercise, a new red color entry should appear.)

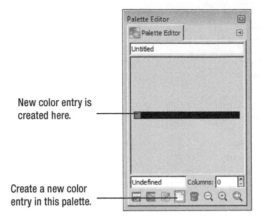

Figure 8-14. *The Palette Editor*

■ **Tip** New entries can also be created by using drag and drop, which currently works best in Linux. Simply click the background color indicator of the toolbox, press and hold the left mouse button, and drag the color onto the Palette Editor.

Becoming a Digital Painter: Using Paint Tools

In this section we will show you how to use the basic paint tools to sketch and paint.

The Eraser Tool

The eraser in GIMP is a basic paint tool. The tool's preliminary function is to change the pixel color to the background color in order to simulate an "erasing" effect. By default, the eraser uses a fuzzy shape for painting.

■ **Tip** Do not confuse the eraser tool with the undo functionality.

How to Erase

To use the full potential of the eraser tool, you will need to understand how the tool works.

1. Create a new image. Verify the two color indicators in the toolbox: the background color indicator should be white and the foreground color indicator black.

2. Change the foreground color to red by clicking on the foreground color indicator in the toolbox. Choose a red color from the color panel in the color dialog and click OK. (If you are unsure about how to do this, see the "Changing the Background Color" exercise.)

3. Select the bucket fill tool from the toolbox.

4. Fill the image with the red foreground color by clicking on the canvas (see Figure 8-15).

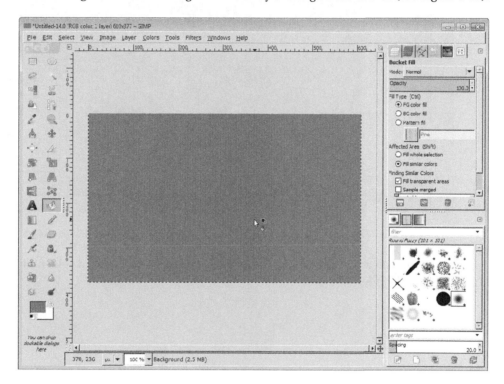

Figure 8-15. *The background color of the canvas after it has been filled with the color red*

5. Select the eraser tool from the toolbox.

6. Draw a line on the red canvas. You should see that the eraser "paints" white because the background color has not been changed and still shows white (see Figure 8-16).

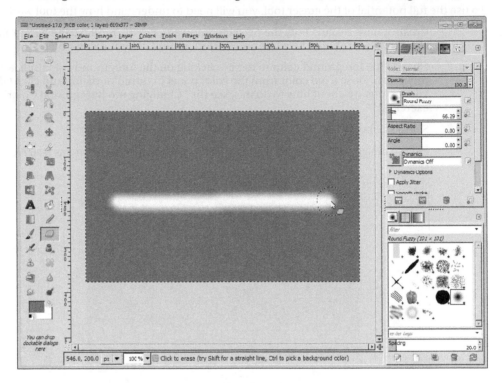

Figure 8-16. *The eraser uses the selected background color, which is white by default*

7. Now change the background color by clicking on the background color indicator. In the color dialog, select a dark color and click OK (see Figure 8-17).

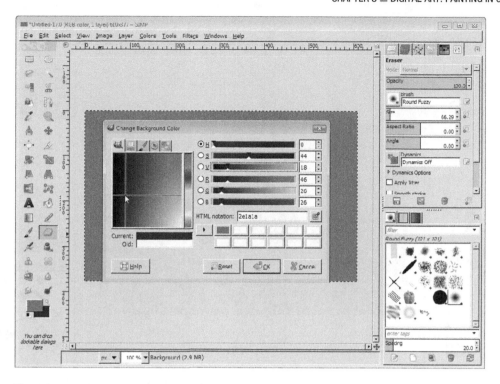

Figure 8-17. *The background color indicator immediately reflects the color selection in the color dialog.*

8. Draw another line on the red canvas. As you can see, now the eraser will paint with a dark background color (see Figure 8-18).

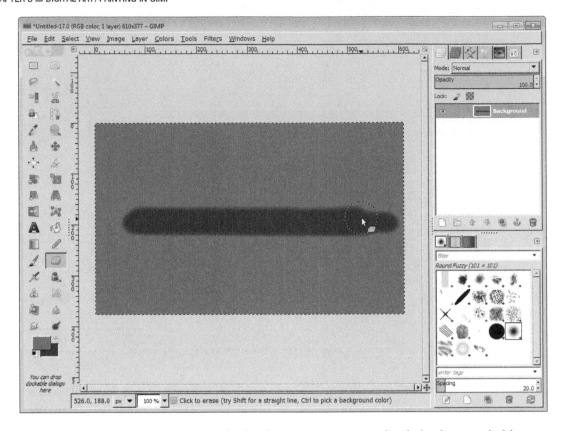

Figure 8-18. *After changing the background color, the eraser now paints with a dark color instead of the default white.*

The Paintbrush Tool

The paintbrush tool uses a soft-edged brush shape by default. Therefore, it is ideal for sketching and painting.

Controlling Your Brush Size, Shape, and Angle

You've already had a quick introduction to the brush and scale tool options. Now it is time to learn more about the tool options and how they can help you paint.

The tool options for the paint tools allow altering how the brush you're painting with behaves in size and shape. If you own a graphics tablet, most of the tool options are controlled by the tablet itself and you can simply start painting. For example, the size of the brush will increase or decrease with the amount of physical pressure you apply to the tablet pen. But still, you need to control the initial size and the shape of your brush.

Brush Shape

The brush option in the tool options dialog allows you to pick a brush shape. This can be compared to the brush that you pick as a painter in real life. It influences how you paint (see Figure 8-19). GIMP provides different brush shapes. You can choose a new brush by clicking on the shape indicator and selecting another brush from the dialog.

The "Doing More with Brushes" section later in this chapter goes into more detail about creating brushes.

Figure 8-19. *Brush comparison of the paintbrush tool (round fuzzy, round, pencil sketch, felt pen, chalk, calligraphic, acrylic)*

Size

The size option allows you to control the size of the brush. This option is the best way to get a very tiny or a very large brush shape to paint with.

Aspect Ratio

With this option, you can twist and bend the brush shape into various degrees, altering the way the brush will paint. Figure 8-20 illustrates how the brush shape changes when you change the aspect ratio in the tool options.

Figure 8-20. *The change of the aspect ratio slider from left to right and how it affects the brush shape*

Angle

The angle controls the rotation of the brush shape. If you select circular brushes, this option will not have a real affect of the brush, because rotating circles will not change the brush. If you choose different brush shapes, you will be able to rotate the brush and influence the painting functionality.

■ **Tip** If you changed a lot of the options in the tool options dialog and you want to return to the GIMP default, use the "Reset to default" icon located on the bottom-right of the tool options dialog. You can also reset all tool options in the Preferences dialog, which you can access through Edit ➤ Preferences.

Sketching

Digital painting is almost similar to painting with real colors on canvas. It is recommended to create a sketch first, before you add any color to your painting and refine it. There is no recommended tool suitable for sketching. Choose either pencil or paintbrush or whatever suits your sketching needs.

1. Create a new canvas with a width and height of 1500 pixels or more by using the Create a New Image dialog (see Figure 8-21).

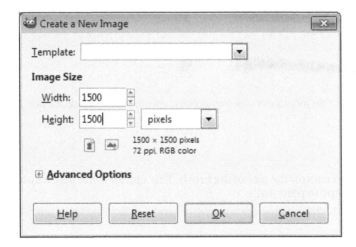

Figure 8-21. *The new image dialog to create a canvas with a bigger size for sketching.*

2. Select the paintbrush tool and open the tool options. If you can't see the tool options dialog, double-click the paintbrush tool icon in the toolbox to open the dialog (see Figure 8-22).

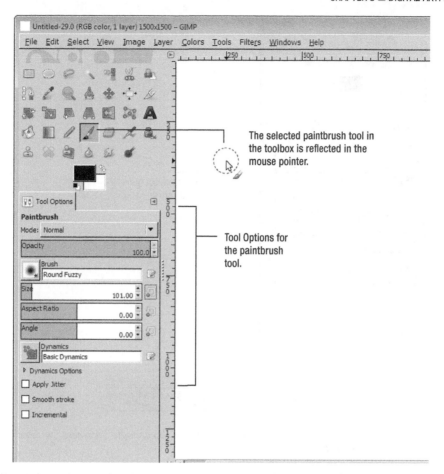

The selected paintbrush tool in the toolbox is reflected in the mouse pointer.

Tool Options for the paintbrush tool.

Figure 8-22. *The size of the brush of the selected paint tool is represented on the canvas.*

3. Verify the brush shape in the paintbrush tool options. The shape of the brush should be set to Round (see Figure 8-23).

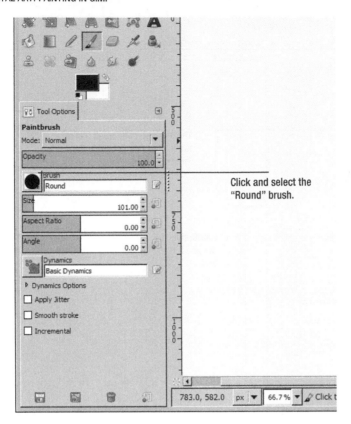

Figure 8-23. *Select the Round brush, as this will give you enough "fuzziness" without making your sketches look dull.*

4. The size of the brush should be very small. You can mark the current value with the mouse and enter "1" or slide the bar to the left with a pressed mouse button (see Figure 8-24). Verify that the Dynamics option is set to "Basic Dynamics" if you use a graphics tablet.

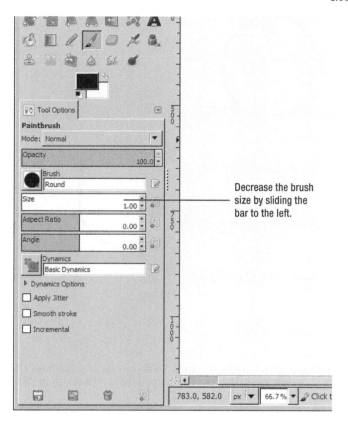

Figure 8-24. *Decreasing the brush size is important, as it will allow you to sketch with a thin line.*

5. Start sketching an object found in your living room or kitchen (for example, an apple or an orange). Keep the sketch very basic and the details to a minimum, like those shown in Figure 8-25.

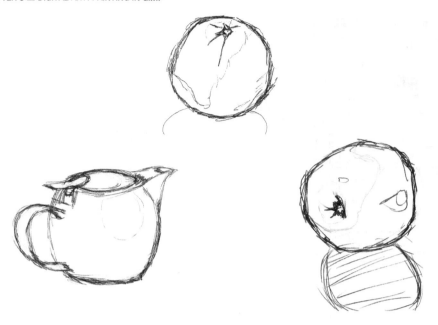

Figure 8-25. *Example sketches*

The sketching abilities of GIMP are limitless. Figure 8-26 shows more advanced sketches you can create. The more you practice sketching, the more you get a feel on how much detail you want to put in your sketches.

Figure 8-26. *Sketches created with more detail.*

Doing More with Brushes

Although GIMP provides a wide range of different brushes for you to paint with, it may be necessary to create your own custom brush shape.

The Brush Selection Dialog

We've already introduced how to select different brush shapes. The brushes dialog is accessible from the paint tool options and allows you to create your own brush shapes (see Figure 8-27). You can obtain the brush selection dialog by selecting Windows ➤ Dockable Dialogs ➤ Brushes or pressing SHIFT+CTRL+B.

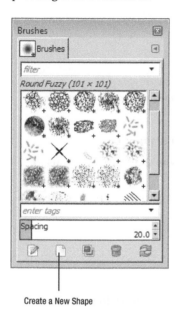

Create a New Shape

Figure 8-27. *The brushes dialog*

■ **Note** The default brush shapes in GIMP cannot be customized. You will need to create your own brush shape.

Create a New Brush Shape

The default brushes shipped with GIMP cannot be edited. If you like to tweak your own artistic brushes, create a copy of an existing brush and change it to fit your own needs.

1. Open the brush selection dialog.

2. Click the "Create new brush" button. The brush editor dialog will appear (see Figure 8-28).

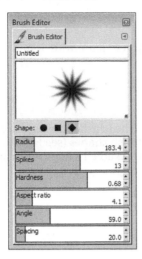

Figure 8-28. *The brush editor dialog showing a newly created, diamond-shaped brush with 13 spikes and a high hardness value*

3. Choose the basic shape of the brush as a circle, square, or diamond.

4. Depending on which brush you're trying to create, play with the editor's options to finalize your brush shape.

5. Switch to the brush selection dialog once you are satisfied with your brush shape. The new brush is automatically saved.

6. Create a new image and try your new brush shape.

Brush Shape Attributes

Figures 8-29, 8-30, and 8-31 show a few, handpicked brush attributes and how they influence the painting style.

Hardness

Software brushes paint more subtly than real brushes. Use a soft brush to create very soft edges or to blend colors. Use a hard brush for outlines of objects.

Figure 8-29. *The difference between a hard and a soft brush.*

Aspect Ratio/Spikes

Spikes attached to brushes paint more artistically than simple, rounded brushes. Use a high aspect ratio to emphasize the spikes more.

Figure 8-30. *A brush with five spikes; the left line uses a small aspect ratio, the right line uses a high aspect ratio*

Spacing

Small spacing creates a seamless line, while big-brush spacing creates dotted lines. You typically want small spacing for sketching and painting.

Figure 8-31. *The difference between a small spacing and a big spacing*

Layers

Layers in GIMP allow you to paint an image with more flexibility. Chapter 6 gave a basic introduction on how to use layers. This section will show you what you need to know about layers specifically for painting.

The Canvas Revised

In the beginning of this chapter, you learned that the "canvas" is a synonym for the digital image that you are painting on.

The canvas in GIMP will provide by default one layer—the background layer. That's why you have two menus in the image menu: Image and Layer. All layers created compose the image.

For example, you can resize the canvas, which will not resize all layers. In turn, you can resize one layer, which will not affect the size of other layers or the size of the image itself.

As shown in Figure 8-32, the size of a layer is always bound by the size of the image; therefore, the size of the digital image on the top of the illustration remains the same, even though one layer is larger than all layers and the image. An image size can be larger than all layers, as shown at the bottom half of Figure 8-32, which results in a larger image, although it can hold smaller-sized layers.

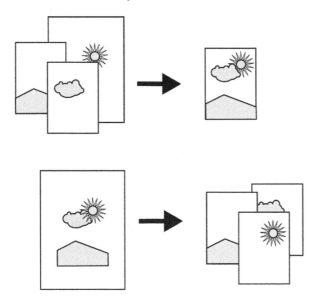

Figure 8-32. *Layers in regard to the digital image, or canvas*

Repositioning the Canvas

You often need to reposition the canvas because you need more space. If you simply start sketching on a blank canvas, you will paint on the background layer.

1. Open one of your sketches. If you don't have one, simply create a new image and use the default width and height of 610 × 377 pixels in the Create a New Image dialog (see Figure 8-33).

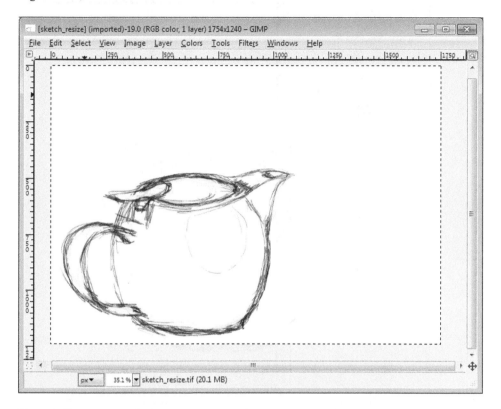

Figure 8-33. *The canvas before repositioning; there is not enough room to add any shadows to the sketched teapot*

2. Select the Move tool from the toolbox window, or press the M key (see Figure 8-34).

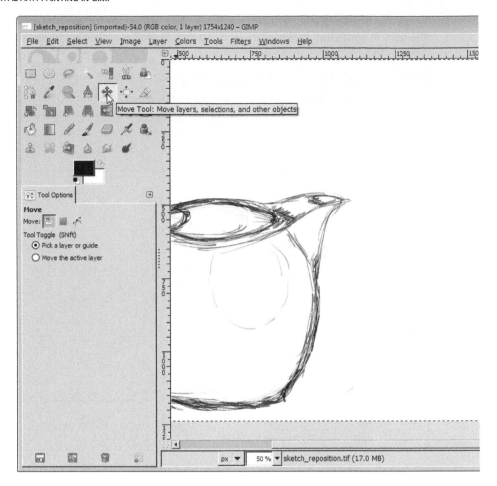

Figure 8-34. *The toolbox with the Move tool selected*

3. Use the Move tool to reposition your image. Click on the image, press and hold the left mouse button, and move the image to where you want it repositioned. Release the left mouse button when you are confident you reached the right position (see Figure 8-35).

Figure 8-35. *Move the canvas in the middle of the image.*

4. You will now see parts of the canvas as a checkerboard and you will not be able to paint. Therefore, you need to resize your canvas to the image size (see Figure 8-36).

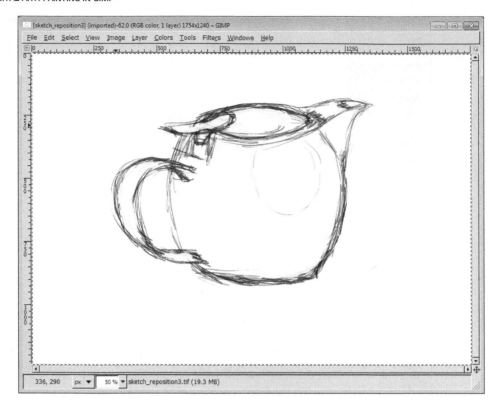

Figure 8-36. *The repositioned canvas after the layer has been resized*

5.   Select Layer ➤ Layer to Image Size.

■ **Note** If you created more than one layer in an image, you can also reduce all layers to one background layer. This is called flattening an image, which will resize any layer in the image. It is a solution if you don't need more than the background layer. To flatten an image, select Image ➤ Flatten Image.

Resizing the Canvas

From time to time, it is necessary to resize the canvas to add more painting space. This can be easily achieved with the Canvas Size dialog.

■ **Note** Scaling will increase or decrease the size of the painting, whereas resizing will add or remove painting space from the image.

1. Open an image or create a new image with the default sizes of 610×377 pixels in the Create a New Image dialog (see Figure 8-37).

Figure 8-37. *The canvas before we resize it; if we want to add more objects to the painting, we will need to add more canvas space.*

2. Resize the canvas by selecting Image ➤ Canvas Size.

3. The dialog allows you to change the canvas size. Increase the size by entering bigger values in the width box. Make sure the chain icon isn't broken because it keeps the aspect ratio of the image (see Figure 8-38).

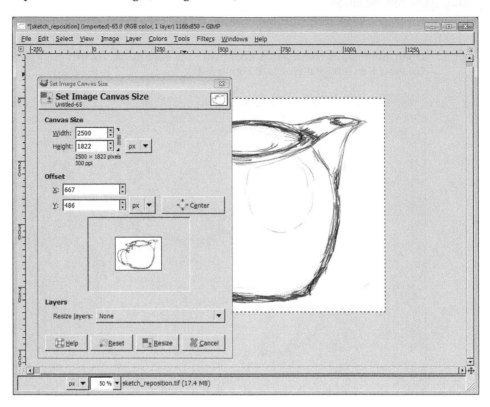

Figure 8-38. *The Set Image Canvas Size dialog*

4. Decide the position of the background layer on the new, resized canvas. Center the background layer by clicking on the Center button.

5. Click the Resize button (see Figure 8-39).

Figure 8-39. *The background layer of the resized canvas has not been resized, so the checkerboard shows*

6. Select Layer ➤ Layer to Image Size (see Figure 8-40).

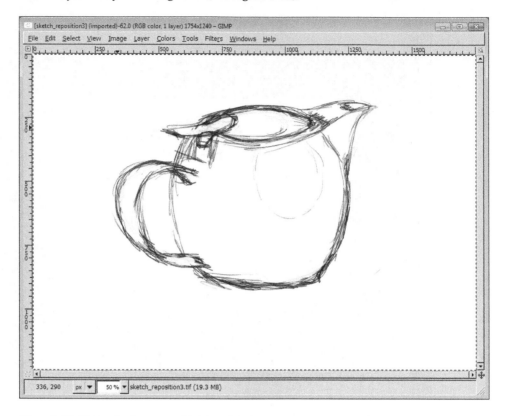

Figure 8-40. *The resized canvas with more painting space*

Managing Layers with the Layer Dialog

The Layers dialog is opened by default when GIMP starts (see Figure 8-41). You can open the layer dialog again by pressing CTRL+l or selecting Windows ➤ Dockable Dialogs ➤ Layers from the image menu. When you create a new image, the layer dialog shows one layer, called Background.

Figure 8-41. *The layer dialog showing the background layer*

The background layer is created with every new canvas. All other layers are added on top of the current selected layer.

Hiding Layers

Layers can be hidden; either by using the eye icon next to the layer title or by reducing the opacity of the layer to a minimum (see Figure 8-42). By hiding layers, you can try different compositions of image elements without exporting them to different images.

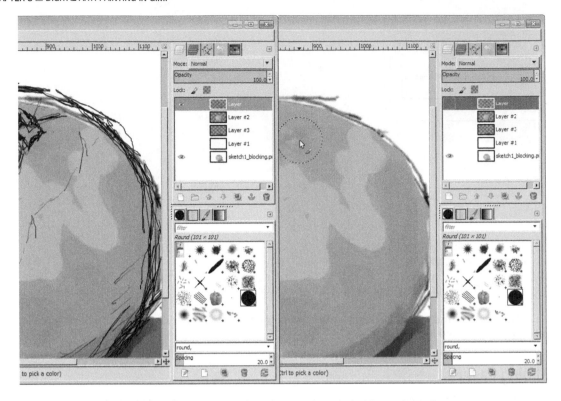

Figure 8-42. *All layers are visible in the left image; the color layer is hidden in the right image*

Coloring Your Sketch

Now that you've learned how to use GIMP to create a sketch, it is now time to apply color to the sketch. Make use of the layer dialog, as this will make it easier to leave your sketch untouched, but try different colors.

1. Create a new image.

2. Create a new layer in the layer dialog. The label should be "sketch" and the fill type should be transparent.

3. Create a new sketch on the newly-created "sketch" layer (see Figure 8-43).

Figure 8-43. *An example sketch to illustrate the coloring process*

4.   Depending on what you want to paint, adding color may not be as easy as it appears. Try to focus on picking the right color and start coloring the biggest areas. (It is advisable to create a new palette for your painting, but not necessary.)

5.   Choose a new foreground color by clicking on the foreground color indicator.

6.   Resize the brush to a medium size in comparison to the painting. Once again, you don't want to paint details.

7.   Create a new layer, name it Color. Move this layer below your sketch layer to use your sketch as a guide (see Figure 8-44).

Figure 8-44. *Apply the color in its own layer, below your sketch; that way you can use your sketch as a guide.*

8. Start applying the color.

9. Pick different shades of the color that you are applying, depending on your painting (see Figure 8-45). If you use a palette, always register the new color in your palette. If you don't use a palette, just use a small color dot in one edge of your painting; that way, you can always pick your color again.

■ **Tip** To quickly toggle between pipette and paint tool, hold CTRL pressed. This will change to the pipette tool with which you can set the foreground color indicator.

Figure 8-45. *The colored sketch without colored details*

Doing More with Layers

Layers can be a very extensive topic in image manipulation, especially because their ability to keep image elements separate makes them so useful. The following sections will show you more advanced uses of layers.

Select the Outline of the Painting

While sketching or applying colors to your painting, it sometimes becomes necessary to select the outline of the painting on a specific layer. To help with this, GIMP provides a selection method called Alpha to Selection.

■ **Note** This method will only work on transparent layers, as GIMP uses transparency to distinguish the outline of the painting from the layer.

---

1. Open the image with the painting that you'd like to use (see Figure 8-46).

Figure 8-46. *Selecting the painting layer (with a transparent background) and the background layer (solid color)*

2. Select the layer from which you would like to perform a selection of the painting outlines.

3. Select on Layer ➤ Transparency ➤ Alpha to Selection. You will now see a selection appear around the painting (see Figure 8-47).

Figure 8-47. *A selection based on the transparency information of the layer, which can be the outline of the painting*

■ **Note** This method will also select half-transparent pixels. You will need to adjust the selection if it happens. See Chapter 9 for more information about how to use selections for drawing.

Exchanging Paintings Between Layers

While painting, it is possible to cut and paste painted elements into other layers. This is very useful, as sometimes you want a strict separation between shadows, colors, and your sketch. With this method, you can rectify mistakes like coloring on the wrong layer.

Before you can exchange paintings between layers, you will need to select your painting.

1. Create a selection of the painting that you would like to exchange.

2. Cut the selected area with either Edit ➤ Cut or CTRL+X (see Figure 8-48).

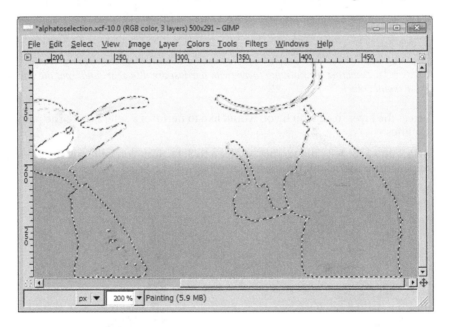

Figure 8-48. *The painting has been cut out; only the selection border remains.*

3. Select the layer that you want to paste the painted area into (see Figure 8-49). This should be a different layer.

Figure 8-49. *The layer labeled "Only Color" is selected and filled with white for demonstration purposes*

4. Remove the selection by choosing Select ➤ None.

5. Paste what you have cut with either Edit ➤ Paste or CTRL+V. A "floating selection" will appear (see Figure 8-50).

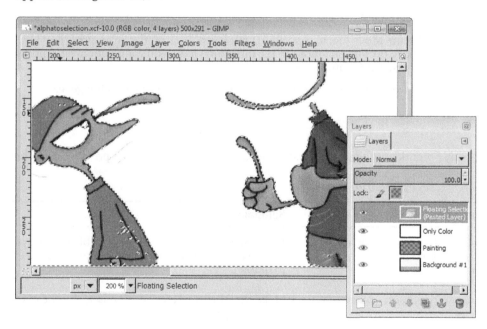

Figure 8-50. *The pasted painting appears as a floating selection in the layer menu. This can be very frustrating for new users who are not aware that it behaves like a layer.*

6. Select the Move tool from the toolbox or choose Tools ➤ Transform Tools ➤ Move.

217

7. Select your painting to move it around by holding your left mouse button pressed. Keep an eye on the layer dialog to be sure you move the correct layer.

8. Anchor the selection by clicking either outside of the floating selection boundaries or by selecting Layer ➤ Anchor Layer.

■ **Note** Anchoring the layer is a very tricky part and needs patience to master it.

Repositioning a Layer

Similar to repositioning a canvas, layers can be repositioned too. Often, you start to sketch out an item on your background or first layer and need to reposition it.

This exercise works best with an image containing more than one layer. You may open one of your previous sketches.

1. Open the layers dialog by selecting Windows ➤ Dockable Dialogs ➤ Layers or pressing CTRL+L.

2. Create a new layer. You should now have at least two layers. Select the top layer. Fill this layer with a dark color using the bucket fill tool.

3. Select the Move tool from the toolbox window or press M.

4. Use the Move tool to reposition your layer. Click on the layer, press and hold the left mouse button, and move in the direction where you want your layer repositioned. Release the left mouse button.

5. Resize your layer to the image by selecting Layer ➤ Layer to Image Size.

Problems with Layers

For any potential problems that may arise regarding layers, Table 8-1 provides quick help tips.

Table 8-1. *Layers Help Tips*

Symptom	Solution
You are unable to paint, no matter which paint tool you choose.	Verify that at least one layer is available in the layer dialog; if not, create a new layer. Check that not all the layers are set to hidden.
You can't paint on transparent areas.	Make sure that the "lock" option is set for the current selected layer.
Whenever I try to move my layer with the move tool, I accidentally move the background layer.	With transparent areas in layers, it is easy to pick the wrong layer with the Move tool. Make sure you select a solid part of the layer not the transparent area.

Filling in the Details

You are constantly picking different colors and different hues of a color to add details to your painting. More detail can be added to the painting by using the paintbrush tool. GIMP provides the following three paint tools to make your life easier:

- **Smudge**: Blends colors

- **Blur/Sharpen**: Refines the depth of objects

- **Dodge/Burn**: Darkens colors or adds highlights

Blending Colors

You started adding colors in the "Coloring your Sketch" exercise.

For the refining task of the sketch you need to know which tools to use to blend colors together. For this task the smudge tool and the blur/sharpen tool can be used. Both tools allow blending colors in a different manner (see Figure 8-51).

Figure 8-51. *Illustration of using the blur tool (left) and the smudge tool (right). The blur tool only blurs the edges of a spot until a maximum, whereas you can smudge edges continuously.*

The blur tool is used to blur edges or make objects of a painting disappear in the background. The smudge tool allows you to blend colors together.

Tool Options: Rate

The blur and smudge tool options has a "Rate" slider at the bottom of the dialog. If you increase the rate, GIMP will blend more colors under the smudge brush. If you decrease the rate, GIMP will, obviously, blend fewer colors. Or, in other words, a smaller rate blends less than a higher rate. Keep that in mind if you want to be very cautious in blending colors together.

How to Blend Colors with the Smudge Tool

This exercise will show you how to blend colors with the smudge tool.

1. Load one of your colored sketches.

2. Choose the smudge tool and slowly smudge the colors together. Add new details in form of new colors and continue smudging.

3. Continue with refining by adding new color. Smudge/blend the colors together until the sketch becomes a seamless shape (see Figure 8-52).

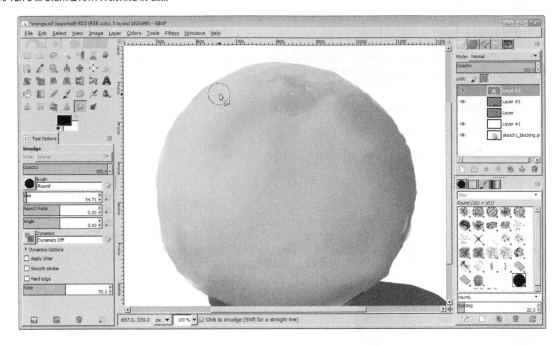

Figure 8-52. *Blending colors with the smudge tool*

Blending colors can be a cumbersome task and may take a long time. You will need patience and practice for this though, as you will start with a "blurry" looking object. Keep on adding details and refine them.

■ **Tip** Use the Lock option in the Layers dialog to prevent smudging your paint into transparent areas. This option is very useful if you divide your painting into separate layers.

Lightening and Darkening Colors

The Dodge/Burn tool is widely used to manipulate the exposure of objects in a photo, but it can also be very useful to manipulate the colors of your painting. The main difference between dodge and burn is that the dodge mode will lighten color areas, whereas the burn mode will darken color areas (see Figure 8-53).

Figure 8-53. *The effects of dodge (left) and burn (right) to add depth to a plain circle*

In Figure 8-53, a "round fuzzy" brush shape was used to add highlights on the left circle, which turns it into a sphere. On the right circle, shadows were added with the burn mode.

Tool Options: Range

Colors can be lightened and darkened at different levels, which is reflected by the range setting in the Dodge/Burn tool options.

- Shadows affect the majority of lighter areas. In dodge mode, colors become "lighter" until they are white. In burn mode, colors become "darker" until they are black.

- Midtones affect the majority of middle tones. In dodge mode, colors get less hue. In burn mode, colors get more hue.

- Highlights affect the majority of darker areas. In dodge mode, colors get less hue. In burn mode, colors get more hue.

■ **Tip** If you are unsure which mode will best fit your needs, stay with the default of the tool, the Midtones option.

What makes this tool so special (compared to other GIMP functionalities) in darkening or lightening an image? You can adjust the pressure and the size and, therefore, control the affected area of the image. Furthermore, the Dodge/Burn tool can be applied accumulatively to paint a gradient from lighter to darker colors.

Re-using Tool Options: The Tool Presets Dialog

If you are frequently changing tools during your painting sessions, the tool presets dialog can be very helpful. Tool Presets is found under Windows ➤ Dockable Dialogs ➤ Tool Presets. For example if you choose a paint brush preset, the brush, the brush size and the brush shape can be preset.

Figure 8-54. *The Tool Presets Dialog*

Choose each preset by clicking on the entry in the dialog. GIMP changes the tool and it's option.

Summary

In this chapter, we introduced you to using GIMP for digital painting. Similar to painting on an actual canvas, we showed you how to create sketches, add color, and make final touches to your painting. The use of layers can be very beneficial to the digital painter. If you don't own a graphics tablet, Chapter 9 will introduce you to digital art using GIMP alone.

CHAPTER 9

■ ■ ■

Digital Art: Drawing in GIMP

Digital art can be created in many different ways, with many different tools. You can create digital art without freehand painting and a graphics tablet. This chapter will show you how you can create digital art with GIMP's tools.

In This Chapter

- How to draw in GIMP
- Draw with selections
- Drawing freely
- Paint without a tablet

How to Draw in GIMP

In principle, all painting tools can be used for drawing, too. How can you create geometric forms with only a mouse and no assistive tools like a drawing pad? It can be achieved by doing any of the following:

- Drawing freehand aided by GIMP (for example, straight lines)
- Creating a selection that reflects any geometric form (for example, circles, ellipses, or squares) and filling or stroking the outline with a paint tool
- Emulating the painting with the dedicated paths tool

You can also refer to Chapter 8, where we introduced every aspect of choosing foreground colors and paint tools, as well as navigating your workspace.

Tools for Drawing

All paint tools under Tools ➤ Paint Tools can be used for drawing. Most of the paint tools are more suitable for painting with a graphics tablet, but the following can be used for drawing with GIMP utilizing a mouse:

- **Pencil**: Draws lines with hard edges

- **Paintbrush**: Draws lines with soft edges

- **Eraser**: Removes strokes or parts of the drawing

- **Airbrush**: Draws fuzzy lines

- **Ink**: Writes calligraphy style lines

- **Bucket Fill**: Fills areas with a color

Size and Shapes

Every paint tool provides tool options, which allow tuning every bit of the paint tool (see Figure 9-1). The size you are drawing with and the shape of the brush will be most important to you.

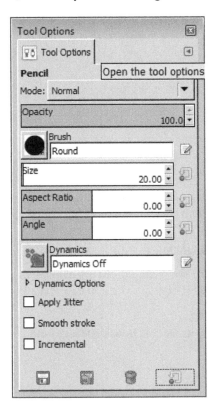

Figure 9-1. The tool options give you quick access to change the shape and size of your current brush.

Changing the Size and Shape of a Paint Tool

The mouse cursor in GIMP always shows a visual representation of the selected paint tool when you move the cursor over the canvas. The selected brush size and shape is also shown (see Figure 9-2). This makes it easy to change the size in the tool options quickly.

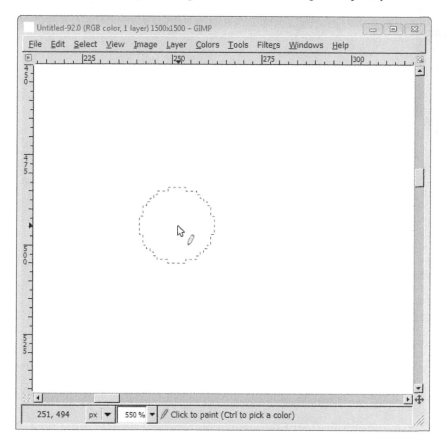

Figure 9-2. *The shape and size of the current brush is displayed when you hover your mouse over the image.*

1. Create a new image.

2. Select a paint tool under Tools ➤ Paint Tools. You can select the Pencil, if you are unsure what to use.

3. Move the mouse cursor over the white area of the canvas. You will notice the helping cursor showing the size of the brush.

4. Open the paint tool options by double-clicking on the tool icon in the toolbox.

5. Slide and change the size entry. For every change, move the cursor over the canvas to see the change of the brush size.

The Bucket Fill Tool

The bucket fill tool allows you to fill areas of your image or selection. It uses the foreground color by default, which is black. The area that is filled is determined by what is bordered by the filling color. This can be the whole image (for example, if the image is white), a selection, or contrast, as illustrated in Figure 9-3.

Figure 9-3. *An area filled with the bucket fill tool. The black-painted pencil lines form a bounding box, which allows you to fill only parts of the image.*

The Eraser Tool

The eraser in GIMP is a basic paint tool. The tool's preliminary function is to change the pixels color to the background color to simulate an "erasing" effect. By default, the eraser uses a fuzzy shape for painting.

■ **Note** Do not confuse the eraser tool with the undo functionality.

How to Erase

Please see page 188 if you are unsure how to use the eraser tool.

Drawing with Selections

Basic geometric figures are created with the help of selections in GIMP. Selections can be filled or stroked. Furthermore, selections can be combined as well as divided, which allows drawing composed geometric figures.

Figures are always drawn by creating new selections and filling them with either a foreground or background color. In Figure 9-4, the selection is created (left) with editable borders; it can still be changing in size and shape. Once you are satisfied with the size and shape, create the selection (middle), and fill it with the bucket fill tool (right) and a selected foreground color.

Figure 9-4. *The process of drawing with selections (from left to right)*

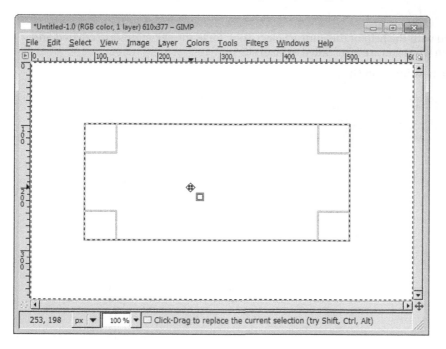

Figure 9-5. *The selection is indicated by alternating black and white stripes, which look like marching ants.*

Selection Tools

Selections are created with the selection tools, which can be found under Tools ➤ Selection Tools in the image menu. All selection tools provide tool options and their behavior can be adjusted.

The following selection tools can be used to create basic geometric figures:

- Rectangle Select

- Ellipse Select

- Free Select (under certain circumstances)

The exercises that follow demonstrate drawing with selections created by the Ellipse Select tool. If you want to create a square selection, the steps are analogous with the Rectangle Select tool.

Creating an Elliptic Selection

Ellipses are created with the help of the Ellipse Select Tool. First, the selections are created and then, depending on what you are after, filled or stroked.

1. Create a new image in GIMP.

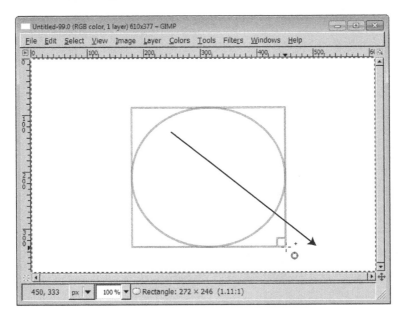

Figure 9-6. An elliptic selection is easily created by drawing an imaginary path (black arrow) by holding the left mouse button.

2. Select the Ellipse Select tool in the toolbox or press E.

3. Create a new selection by clicking and holding the mouse button while you drag the mouse to either side of the image (see Figure 9-6). A helping square is displayed around the selection. If you are satisfied, click the image again to create the selection. You will now see a selection with "marching ants" surrounding the selection (see Figure 9-7).

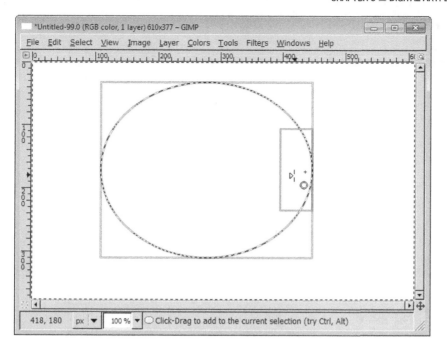

Figure 9-7. *Hover your mouse pointer over the edges of the selection to see the helping square.*

4. To draw an elliptic outline, choose Select ➤ Border. Type in the size of the border and click OK. Fill the created border with the bucket fill tool by clicking in the border (see Figure 9-8 and Figure 9-9).

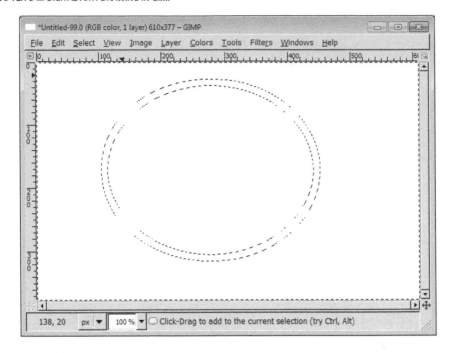

Figure 9-8. *A border is easily created around the ellipsis.*

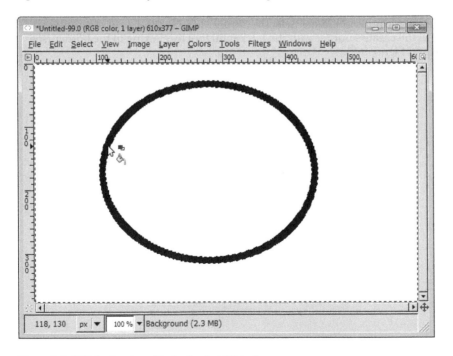

Figure 9-9. *Fill the border with the bucket fill tool.*

Mullica Hill Branch
856-223-6060

Title: GIMP for absolute
beginners
Date due: 11/27/2017,23:
59

Ask a Librarian
856-223-6050
****

ww.gcls.org
223-6060

Creating a Circle

Circles are created with elliptic selections. The following exercise alters an elliptic selection into a circle by locking the aspect ratio.

1. Create a new elliptic selection with the Ellipse Selection tool described in the section "Create an Elliptic Selection".

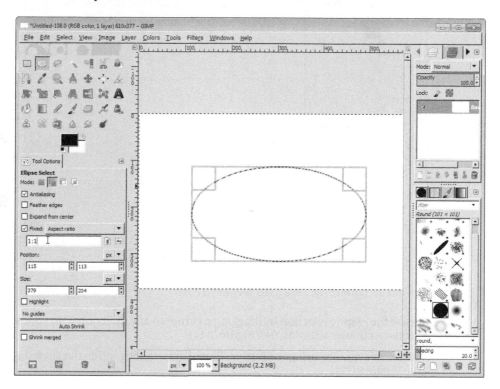

Figure 9-10. *By locking in the aspect ratio by 1:1 in the selection tool options, you can create even-sized selections, such as circles.*

2. Open the tool option dialog of the Ellipse Selection tool. Select the option labeled Fixed:, which should be set to "Aspect ratio" by default.

3. Type an aspect ratio of 1:1, as shown in the entry box in Figure 9-11.

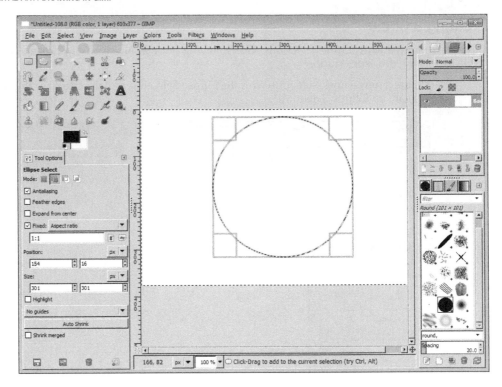

Figure 9-11. *By resizing, the ellipsis becomes a circle.*

4. Resize the elliptic selection by dragging a corner to any direction with your mouse. You created a circular selection (see Figure 9-11).

5. Fill the selection by using the bucket fill tool and clicking inside the circled selection (see Figure 9-12).

Figure 9-12. *Fill the selection by using the bucket fill tool.*

Doing More with Selections

Basic selections can be combined with new selections. You can create many different shapes with that in mind.

Selection Modes

Each selection tool can be set to a specific mode. The default mode is set to "Replace the current selection." This always creates a new selection to avoid confusion.

Figure 9-13. *A variety of selection modes illustrated from top to bottom: add, subtract, and intersect. Two circle selections for each mode have been filled.*

You will most likely practice with different selection modes in order to create composed geometric objects and to get familiar with the modes benefits. The following exercise will help you start playing with the selection modes.

Creating Composed Forms with Selections

This exercise uses two modes: combine and subtract.

1. Create a new image in GIMP.

2. Create a new selection, as described in the "Creating a Circle" section.

3. Open the tool options for the selection tool by double-clicking on the tool icon in the toolbox.

4. Switch the selection mode to "Add to the current selection."

5. Draw a new selection that overlaps the current selection. Create the selection with a single mouse-click (see Figure 9-14).

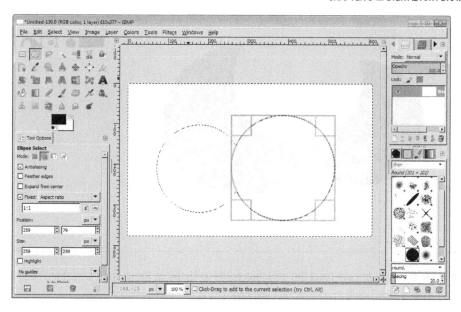

Figure 9-14. *Create a new selection next to the first circle to let it overlap.*

6. Focus on the tool options again. Now you will remove part of the selection by switching the selection mode to "Subtract from the current selection."

7. Draw a new selection that overlaps the current selection (see Figure 9-15).

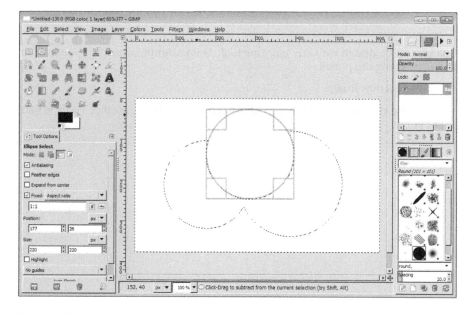

Figure 9-15. *In subtract mode, the new selection creates a circular "hole."*

8. Create an outline or fill the selection (see Figure 9-16).

Figure 9-16. *Use the bucket fill tool to fill the selection.*

■ **Tip** Make sure you always reset the selection mode to "Replace the current selection," because other selection modes may result in undesirable selections in later GIMP sessions.

Drawing Freely

GIMP provides helping hands if you are drawing freely to create simple geometric figures.

Drawing a Straight Line

Straight lines can be drawn with any painting tool. As an example, we show you how to draw a straight line by using the pencil.

1. Create a new image.

2. Choose the pencil or paint tool of your choice. Press N or select Tools ➤ Paint Tools ➤ Pencil.

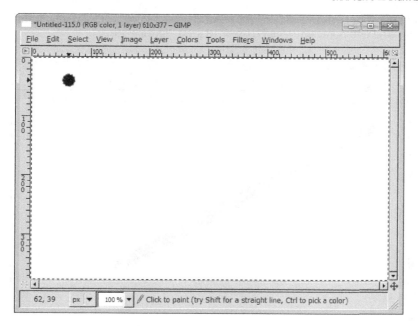

Figure 9-17. *A straight line starts with a single point, which you create with a single mouse-click.*

3. With a single mouse-click, create the first point of the line somewhere on the canvas (see Figure 9-17).

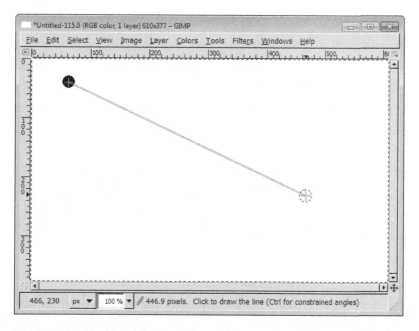

Figure 9-18. *While you hold the Shift key, a line connects the mouse pointer and the first point.*

4. Hold the Shift key while making the second point, which, with a single mouse-click, marks the end of the line (see Figure 9-18 amd Figure 9-19).

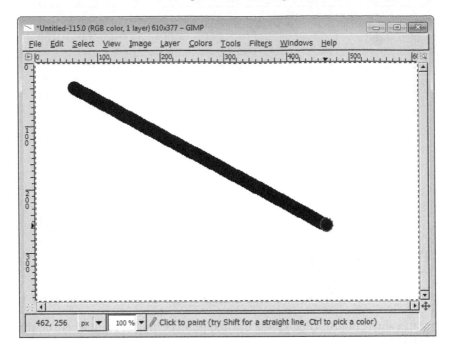

Figure 9-19. *A straight line made by holding the Shift key*

■ **Tip** You can create consecutive line segments by simply continuously creating points with a mouse click on the canvas, while holding the SHIFT key pressed.

Pixel Art

Chapter 3 introduced the pixel—the smallest element in a digital image. Pixel art is a digital art form using the smallest element in an image. This art originates from the early forms of computer graphics. It was used for icons in operating systems and games. The art form is based on the pixel, which makes it distinguishable from a real-world painting because printouts can look blocky. The art is now used in all kinds of computer application icons. The images can either look flat or mimic a 3D effect, which is called isometric.

What to Avoid

Before creating your first pixel art masterpiece, there is one hint you should follow: avoid creating jagged lines. Pixels placed symmetrically are rendered crisp on your display; the eye picks up misplaced pixels very easily. Lines can look jagged and the image will not look nice (see Figure 9-20).

Figure 9-20. *Close up, the pixels that compose the lines are not symmetrical (illustrated in red), which will give a jagged or uneven impression from a distance.*

What to Draw

Diagonal lines drawn with the same number of pixels look sharper and crisper. Art composed of symmetrical aligned pixels will look nice and crisp (see Figure 9-21).

Figure 9-21. *If you create diagonal lines, draw the diagonal increment with the same number of pixels.*

Using Depth in Pixel Art

Isometric pixel art uses the isometric perspective to create images with depth. Most of these images had a part in early computer games. The images are very small, similar to icons, which allow you to put a lot of detail into the art—making them almost look like toys.

Figure 9-22 illustrates why it is important to arrange pixels symmetric. The image on the left uses symmetric arranged pixels which lead to a very clean and crisp image on the display. The image on the right uses asymmetrically-arranged pixels, which leads to a distorted image.

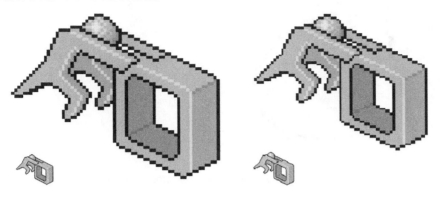

Figure 9-22. *Pixel art with depth added to it, also called an isometric view*

Drawing a Simple Isometric Box

Drawing a box is the simplest geometric object. Most geometric forms in isometric pixel art use a box as its imaginary base model.

Basically, you create the frame, color the frame, and add highlights and shadows.

1. Create a blank, white canvas with File ➤ New.

2. Choose the Pencil tool and open the tool options. Verify that the pencil tool size option is set to the lowest setting (1.00) and a Round Brush shape is chosen. Set the Dynamics option to "Dynamics Off" because you need a hard-painting pencil. (The "Size and Shapes" section at the beginning of this chapter can show you how to do that.)

3. Because you may use the eraser often, make sure you have set the Eraser tool to the lowest brush size (1.00). With this tool also, set the Dynamics option to "Dynamics Off."

4. Set the zoom level to the highest setting: View ➤ Zoom ➤ 16:1. While drawing, you can constantly switch back to the normal zoom level to see the pixel drawing evolving.

5. Choose a black foreground color. (This should be the default.)

6. Start drawing a simple square (see Figure 9-23).

Figure 9-23. *Start by drawing the front side of the box.*

7. Create diagonal lines to add depth to the square (see Figure 9-24).

240

Figure 9-24. *If you start with pixel art, draw the diagonal lines pixel by pixel.*

The box is now almost finished, but the coloring can make the difference between a dull object and a sophisticated-looking object. You will continue now by adding highlights and shadows to the box.

8. Choose a color to fill two sides of the box. Depending on where you imagine the light will come from, leave one box for a darker color—the shadowed part of the box (see Figure 9-25).

Figure 9-25. *Fill the sides of the boxes with the bucket fill tool.*

9. Choose a darker color and fill the final side of the box with this darker color (see Figure 9-26).

Figure 9-26. *One side will be darker to simulate a shadow.*

10. Choose a lighter color and redraw the inner edge sides. This will make the box look "plastic" (see Figure 9-27).

Figure 9-27. *Paint the inner edges of the box with a brighter color; this creates a plastic look.*

11. If you want to make the edges shinier, tip the edge with a very bright, almost white color.

Figure 9-28. *To make the corner shiny, use a very bright color that is almost white.*

12. Set the zoom level to 100% to see the box in a normal size.

Creating a Simple Isometric House

As a final example, we will show you how to create a simple house. You should be able to extend your virtual world from there.

1. Create a new image in GIMP.

2. Choose the Pencil tool, scale the brush size to the lowest setting (1.00), and make sure you do this with the Eraser tool as well. Choose the highest zoom option. (See the "Drawing a Simple Isometric Box" tutorial to prepare your working area.)

3. Create a new transparent layer in the layer dialog. It will help you keep your drawing off the background so that you can paint the background independently (for example, place your house on the moon?)

4. Draw the outlines of the house by using two pixels. This will be much like drawing a simple box, depending on the shape of the house.

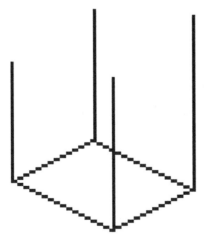

Figure 9-29. *Start by drawing the frame of the house.*

5.   Create a new layer. This will be used for drawing the roof. Because the roof will be tilted slightly upwards, you need a layer to toy around with drawing pixels. It will also be easier for you to position the roof on top of the house with the Move tool (see Figure 9-30).

■ **Note** Positioning transparent layers with thin lines is tricky because you need to pick the exact position of the line otherwise, the Move tool picks the background layer by default. A high zoom will make this operation easier.

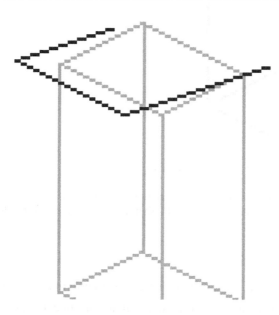

Figure 9-30. *Reduce the opacity of the background layer (the box) to assist in positioning the roof correctly while stilling drawing the black pixels for the roof.*

6.   So far we used two pixels for the side lines. Try to use three or four pixels for the roof lines to create the impression of being more angular. Again, this is up to you and what you find looking good (see Figure 9-31).

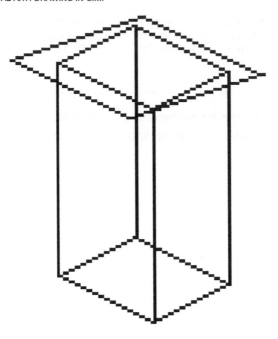

Figure 9-31. *The basic structure of the house without coloring*

7. Use the Move tool to move around the roof in case you need to reposition it. You may still need to make a few adjustments, but you can also do so during or after coloring the image.

Coloring

After you established the outline of the house, you color it and add highlights and shading.

1. Choose a color for the house. If you like a house that is made of wood, choose a brownish foreground color.

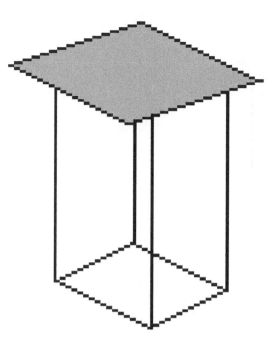

Figure 9-32. *Coloring, started with the roof*

2. Start by filling the roof of the house with a color (for example, choose brown for wood). (See Figure 9-32.) Because you have created the roof on its own layer, you can fill the complete roof area without taking care of intersecting lines. Continue by also filling the sides of the house. If the door is shut, also fill the front side with a color.

3. Add highlights to draw the wood. Use the Pencil and choose a brighter version of the foreground color. Paint horizontal lines every three or four pixels. Use the straight line technique from "Drawing a Straight Line" (see Figure 9-33).

■ **Tip** When drawing with the Pencil tool, you can quickly select the foreground color by holding the CTRL key and clicking on the pixel you want the foreground color to match.

Figure 9-33. *Bright and dark lines next to each other simulate depth.*

4. Choose a darker version of the foreground color and paint straight lines next to the brighter lines. This creates a depth effect.

5. Now concentrate on the roof and create the same effect by using a brighter color and a darker color (see Figure 9-34).

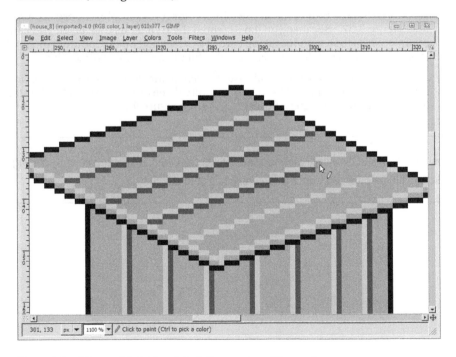

Figure 9-34. *Diagonal bright and dark lines on top of the roof*

6.   From here on, you can add little details to finish your picture. Add birds, grass, or whatever you can think of (see Figure 9-35).

Figure 9-35. *The finished pixel image with details added*

Painting Without a Tablet

Chapter 8 describes how you can use all aspects of your graphics tablet to paint whatever you imagine. You can also do this without a graphics tablet with the help of the Paths tool. It allows stroking lines and emulating paint dynamics, which are usually performed with your free hand.

Assistive Painting: The Paths Tool

The path tool allows you to create smooth curves and complex geometric objects. This makes it the perfect tool for drawing and creating selections for image manipulation.
The advantages of using paths include the following:

*   You can create curvy lines, as well as straight lines, like the Pencil tool.

*   Selections can be transformed into paths and paths can be transformed into selections. This is needed to fill drawings with a color when created with a path.

*   Paths are saved with the GIMP Image Format (XCF) and can therefore be reused when reopening the image. This is a good way to save selections as well.

The paths tool can be selected from the toolbox or by pressing the B key. It has many different modes, which makes it a tool for the moderately advanced user. Every line segment uses handles to bend the line segment in every direction. These lines are called paths or vectors.

Anatomy of a Path

A path line can also be referred to as a path segment because it is not a simple straight line connected by two points. The path uses handles and anchors to create a curve out of a path. Think of it as attaching weights to a wooden plank to make it bend (see Figure 9-36).

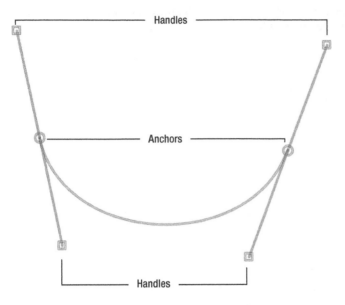

Figure 9-36. *An anatomy of a path. The handles on the anchors are used to bend the path by dragging the handles.*

Creating a Path Segment

A simple path segment is created similar to a straight line. You create two points and GIMP connects the two points with a path. This exercise does not end by creating a path segment.

The path tool's primary use is to create curves and stroke them with a paint tool of your choice. Paths can be altered at any time before you stroke the path, which provides a lot of flexibility.

1. Create a new image.

2. Choose the path tool or simply press B.

3. Create a first point with a single mouse-click somewhere in the image.

4. Create another point somewhere else in the image to connect the anchor points and to create the line (see Figure 9-37).

Figure 9-37. *A path segment created with two anchor points*

Creating an S-Curve

An S-Curve is a simple form of a curve, where the two handles of the anchor points face opposite directions.

1. Create a new image or use the path from the previous exercise.

2. Bisect the line (use your imagination) and move your mouse pointer to the first half of the path.

3. Drag the path slowly in one direction, which is illustrated in Figure 9-38. The closer your mouse pointer is to an anchor point, the greater the increase of the curve.

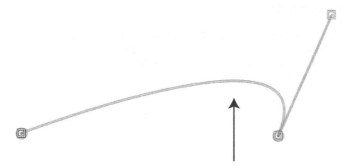

Figure 9-38. *Drag the line segment in the direction indicated by the arrow.*

4. Now do the same with the opposite half of the path segment. Move the segment towards the opposite direction, as shown in Figure 9-39.

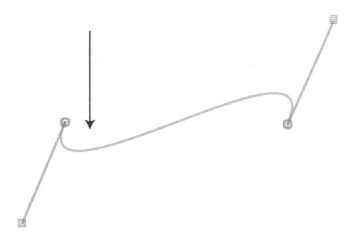

Figure 9-39. *To create an S-shape, move the other half of the path in the opposite direction.*

5. You can now use the handles to shape the line further. Simply click the little squares at the end of the handle and drag them into different positions to see how the handle influences the curve and to get a feeling for the path tool.

Creating an M-Shaped Curve

An M-shaped curve involves a bit more bending of the curve. It uses at least three anchor points and two path segments.

1. Create a new image.

2. Create two path segments by creating three anchor points (see Figure 9-40).

Figure 9-40. *A path with two segments*

3. Move the entire left path segment upwards, as illustrated in Figure 9-41, by holding your mouse button and moving the mouse forward. You decide which part of the path that you move upwards. Move the path segment in the middle upwards and you will create a nice, circular-shaped path.

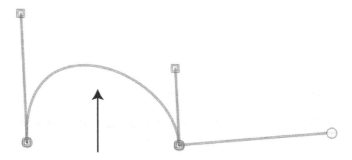

Figure 9-41. *Move the entire path segment upwards.*

4. Move the second path segment upwards, as illustrated in Figure 9-42.

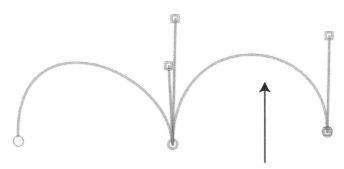

Figure 9-42. *The second path segment is moved upward to create an M-shaped path.*

Deleting Anchor Points and Path Segments

When creating paths, it may be necessary to delete obsolete anchor points.

Deleting path segments always involves deleting their connecting anchor points, as shown in Figures 9-43 and 9-44. With the anchor points deleted, the corresponding path segment will be removed. Path segments can be easily deleted by selecting an anchor point and by hitting Delete on your keyboard.

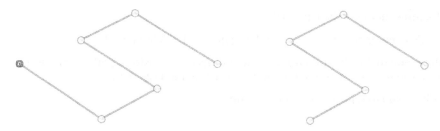

Figure 9-43. *If you delete an anchor point on either edge of the path, the path segment connecting the anchor will be deleted.*

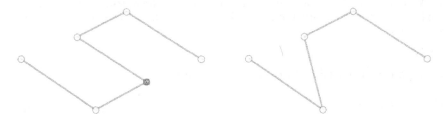

Figure 9-44. *If you delete a path segment inside the path, the next anchor point will be used to reconnect the path.*

The Path Tool Options

The tool options of the path tool provide three modes affecting path creation, movement, and deletion of anchor points. Each of the modes allows various choices to be made, which makes the tool quite complex.

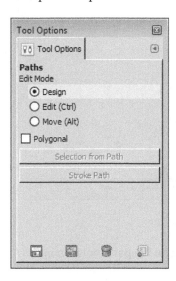

Figure 9-45. *The path tool options showing the three edit modes*

The following are the three modes of the path tool:

- **Design**: Adds new anchor points and path segments (the default mode)
- **Edit**: Allows you to drag handles from anchor points and transform path segments; it also allows you to insert new anchor points in existing path segments
- **Move**: Allows you to reposition the entire path

Closing a Path

So far, we've showed you how to create simple paths. What if you want to draw an object such as an ellipsis or a cube? What if you want to trace a portrait? The path you draw needs to be closed the same way a circle is closed: the end point and start point are merged. This exercise shows you how to created closed paths.

1. Create a new image

2. Create a new path, which needs to be closed (see Figure 9-46).

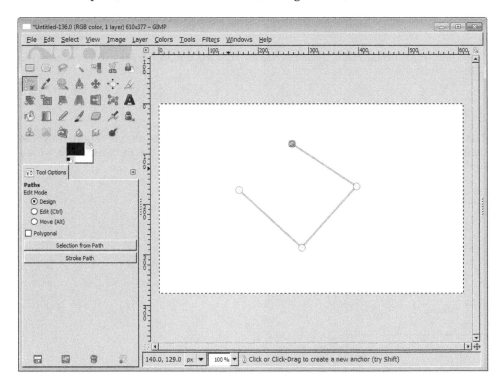

Figure 9-46. *A new path is created, which we would like to close.*

3. Open the tool options of the path tool by double-clicking on the path tool icon in the toolbox or by pressing B.

4. Change the path tool to edit mode (see Figure 9-47).

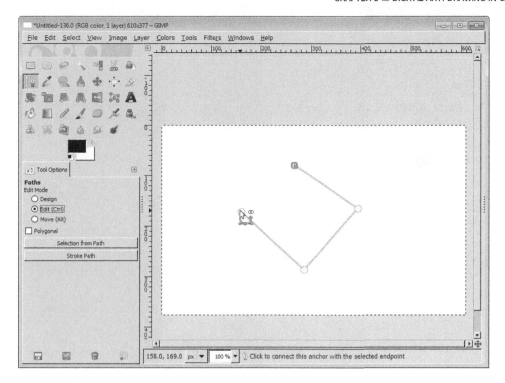

Figure 9-47. *The path tool options need to be in edit mode to connect the start and endpoint.*

5. To close the path click the first anchor point that you created (see Figure 9-48).

253

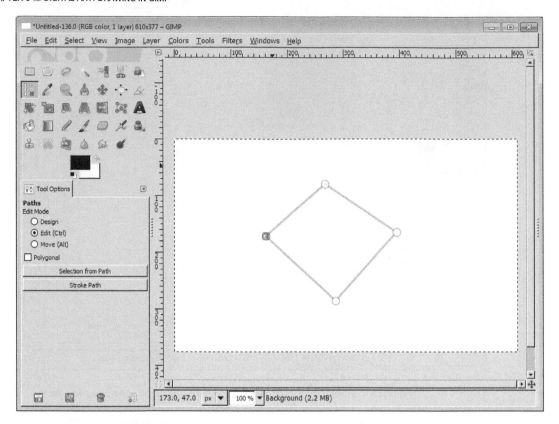

Figure 9-48. *The closed path*

Stroking a Path with a Paint Tool

So far, the path is not more than a reference line, which is invisible when you save your picture. Once the path has been created, it is time to stroke it with the paint tool of your choice. By clicking the "Stroke Path" button, which can be found in the path tool options, a Stroke Path dialog appears (see Figure 9-49).

Figure 9-49. *The Stroke Path dialog lets you render the paths you created. The options allow you to use any paint tool or a simple line.*

This dialog allows you to choose how your path becomes visible; or, in other words, painted on the canvas.

1. Create a new image.

2. Open the tool options of the path tool by double-clicking on the path tool icon in the toolbox.

3. Create a new path and click the Stroke Path button in the path tool options dialog or select Edit ➤ Stroke Path (see Figure 9-50).

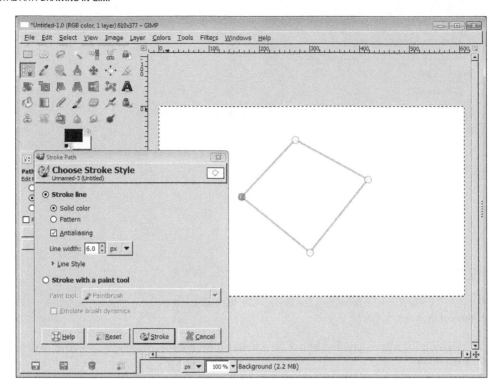

Figure 9-50. *Drawing the created path with the Stroke Path dialog is easy because it strokes the paths you created with a normal line style.*

4. Choose the paint tool you'd like to stroke the path with and click Stroke (see Figure 9-51).

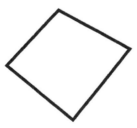

Figure 9-51. *After the path has been stroked, the resulting image will look like this illustration.*

Common Problems with Using Paths

Using paths is a very advanced technique. Table 9-1 lists common pitfalls and how to manage them.

Table 9-1. *Symptoms and solutions*

Symptom	Solution
When I move one anchor point, the whole path moves.	This can happen after you bend the path. Two anchor points or more are selected. You deselect one anchor point by holding the Shift key.
I can't seem to add any anchor points anymore.	Check if the "mode" option in the path tool options is set to Design.
I always create additional anchor points by accident.	Simply delete them by changing the "mode" option in the path tool options to Edit. Hold the Shift key and click the anchor point you want to delete.
I can't bend paths anymore.	Check if the Polygonal option is set in the path tool options and uncheck it if it is.

The Paths Dialog

The Paths dialog can be opened by selecting Windows ➤ Dockable Dialogs ➤ Paths (see Figure 9-52). It provides a way to manage all paths that have been created for the currently opened image. New entries in the dialog are created if you create new paths in your image.

The dialog can also be used to export and import paths to exchange information with vector drawing applications like Inkscape or Adobe Illustrator in a vector file format called SVG.

Figure 9-52. *The paths dialog, with one unnamed created path in the list*

Turning a Selection into a Path

We've already shown you in previous sections how to create a selection. Sometimes it can be helpful to save a selection for later use.

1. Create a new image in GIMP.

2. Create a selection with a selection tool (see Figure 9-53). (If you are unsure follow section "Create an Ellipsis.")

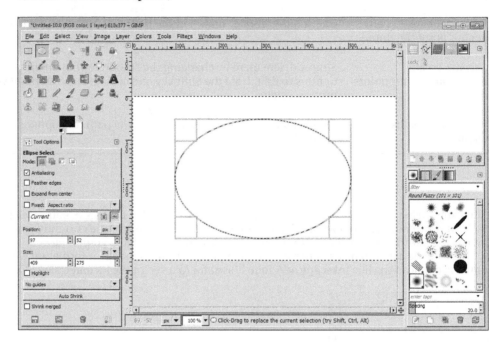

Figure 9-53. *An elliptic selection to convert to a path. The right panel shows in the top-left corner of the paths dialog.*

3. Click Select ➤ To Path to create a path from the selection (see Figure 9-54).

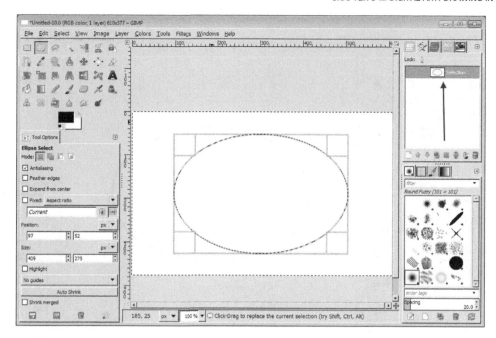

Figure 9-54. *The selection still exists, but the paths dialog now shows a new entry (illustrated by the long arrow).*

4. De-select the selection by clicking Select ➤ None.

5. Open the path dialog (Windows ➤ Dockable Dialogs ➤ Paths). You should now see a new entry in the dialog (see Figure 9-54).

6. To stroke this path, focus on the path dialog. Choose the button "Paint along the path" (second button from right), which will bring up the Stroke Path dialog (see Figure 9-55).

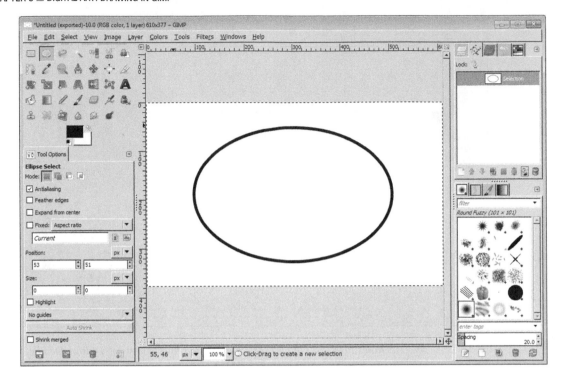

Figure 9-55. *The stroked path that was originally created out of a selection*

Turning a Path into a Selection

If you like to reuse saved selections from before or like to extract elements from a photo, create the path and transform it into a selection.

1. Create a new image in GIMP.

2. Create a new path. You don't have to close the path, which is described in the "Closing a Path" section. If you don't close the path, GIMP creates the selection from the first anchor point to the end point (see Figure 9-56).

Figure 9-56. *Create the path around the object; here it starts at the bottom of the t-shirt.*

3. Click Select ➤ From Path to create a selection from the path (see Figure 9-57).

Figure 9-57. *Once the path is finished, the selection is easily created.*

4. Optional: You can now extract part of the image by using Edit ➤ Cut and paste it as a new layer by using Edit ➤ Paste as ➤ New Layer (see Figure 9-58).

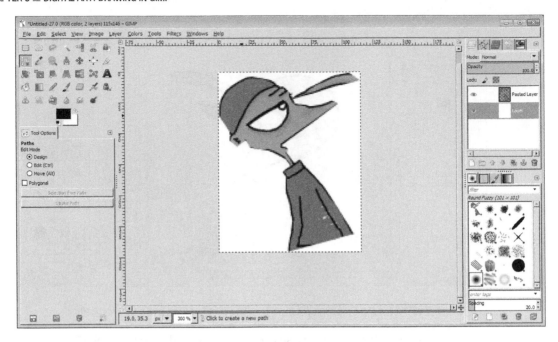

Figure 9-58. *The extracted and pasted image as a new layer (the selection was not very precise on the edges of the image)*

Extracting Elements from an Image with a Path

The Path tool can become very useful to extract elements from photos. You create a path, transform it into a selection, and copy the image element you want to extract. This method shows a different way of extracting elements. GIMP also provides the Foreground Selection Tool, which can be found in Tools ➤ Selection Tools ➤ Foreground Select.

1. Open the image that holds the element you'd like to extract. For this exercise, we will reuse the example image we've used in the previous example and refine the selection.

2. Create a new path around the object you'd like to select. Focus on creating a rough outline (see Figure 9-59).

Figure 9-59. *Create a rough outline with the path.*

3. Set the zoom to the maximum, or depending how many anchor points you have set, a zoom level you can comfortably work with. Now customize the path by bending the segments to shape a form around the object you want to extract. Click and hold the mouse button while dragging the segments. Figure 9-60 illustrates this by using arrows.

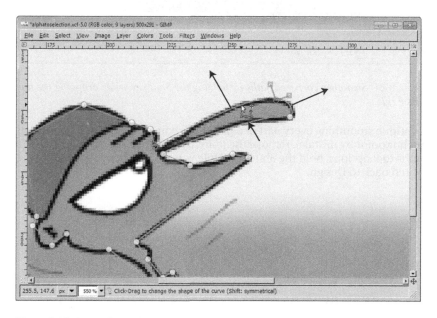

Figure 9-60. *Move the paths in the direction you want to bend them.*

4. For paths segments that form a corner, you can smooth them by holding the Shift key while clicking and dragging the handles in either direction (see Figure 9-61).

■ **Tip** To navigate better in high zoom levels, hold the spacebar while moving your mouse pointer around.

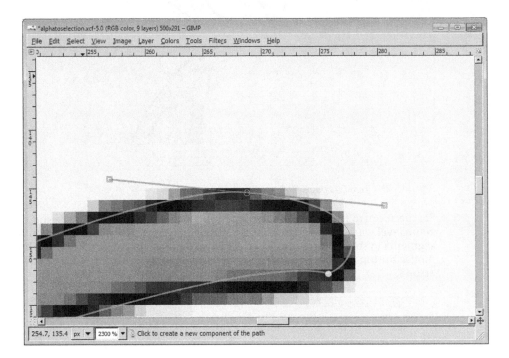

Figure 9-61. *Smoothen cornered paths by holding the Shift key while dragging the handles to either side.*

5. Continue smoothing every part of a path until you are satisfied. If you added another anchor point by mistake, remove the point by changing the path mode to Edit in the paths tool options, hold the Shift key while you click on the point. Make sure you switch back to Design.

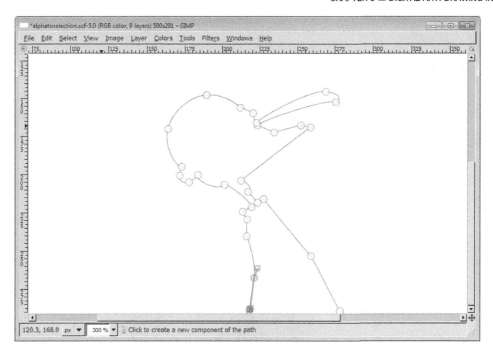

Figure 9-62. *The path after it has been "smoothened" manually*

6. Create a selection by clicking Select ➤ From Path (see Figure 9-62).

7. Extract the element by copying it to the clipboard with Edit ➤ Copy or CTRL + C.

8. You can now use your extracted element in a new image by selecting File ➤ Create ➤ From Clipboard (see Figure 9-63).

Figure 9-63. *The extracted image now looks much better. With paths you have full control and you can readjust and refine the paths to make the extractions even better.*

Creating Text That Flows Along a Path

Chapter 6 introduced the text tool to create a web banner. Text usually flows naturally from one direction to the other. But if you are creating invitations or cards to celebrate your child's birthday, for example, you will need something more out of the line: text that follows a curve, for example. With the path tool, you can create the foundation for the text direction; the path tool provides the text itself. Using them together, you can create interesting word art.

1. Create a new image in GIMP.

2. Create a new path with two segments. Don't bend the path for now; concentrate on the basic shape (see Figure 9-64).

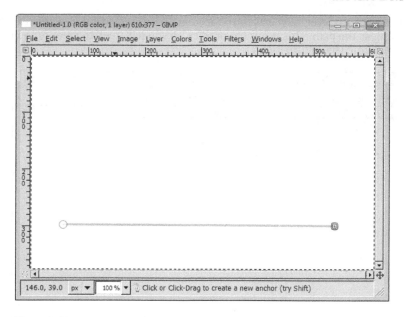

Figure 9-64. *Create a very basic shape.*

3. Bend the path to the shape. Simply drag the path upwards with the mouse to a semicircle shape. The text will later flow over and under the path (see Figure 9-65).

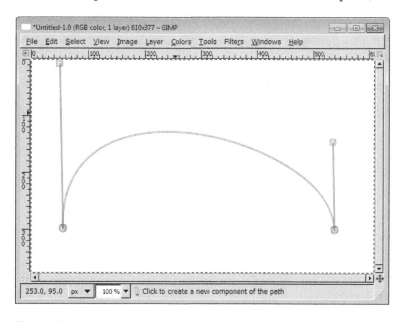

Figure 9-65. *After bending the path segment it may not look symmetrical. Fix that by simply pushing one of the helping lines up- or downwards.*

4. Create a new text layer (as it was introduced in Chapter 6). Mind you, the text should be as long as the path. This is hard to predict, so you will need to cater for a little trial-and-error time (see Figure 9-66).

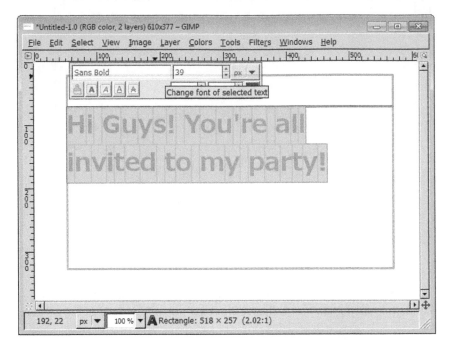

Figure 9-66. *After creating the initial text, make it larger (if you need) by selecting the text and changing the text size.*

5. Once the text is created, select Layer ➤ Text along Path. GIMP creates a new path with the text information along the old path. To avoid any confusion, disable the visibility of the text layer by clicking the eye icon next to the layer entry (see Figure 9-67).

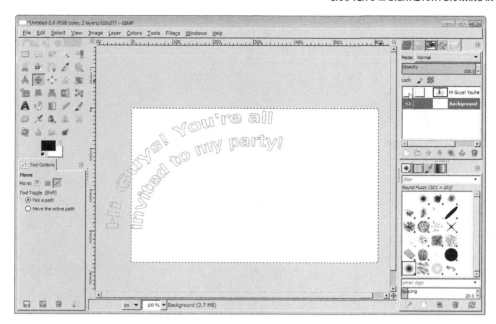

Figure 9-67. *GIMP rendered the text along the path and the visibility of the text layer is switched off.*

6. Check your path dialog and you will see a new path entry. The text rendered along the path is itself a path. This is important, as you still need to render the new text to the layer, otherwise nothing will show up in the printout.

7. If your path is not rendered correctly, you may need to remove the path in the path dialog, change the text and re-render it along the path again. If it is rendered out of the image (in the gray area), you may need to move the path into the image (see Figure 9-68). To do that, select the move tool and open the move tool options. By default you will move the layer, but you will want to move the text rendered along the path.

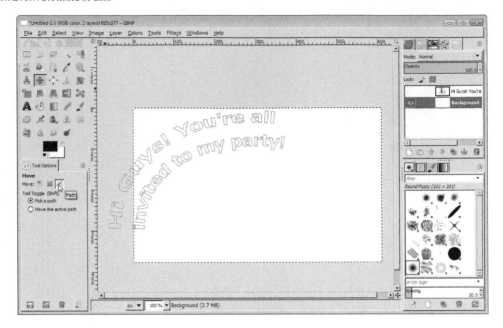

Figure 9-68. *The text is rendered over the edges of the image.*

8. Check the layer dialog. Select the background layer to stroke the text rendered along the path.

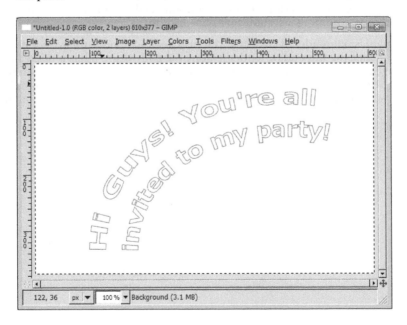

Figure 9-69. *The path moved to the middle of the image with the move tool*

9. Now it is up to you: you can stroke the path with the paint tool and color of your choice as introduced in the "Stroking a Path with a Paint Tool" section (see Figure 9-70). You can also fill the path by creating a selection introduced in the "Creating a Selection from a Path" section (see Figure 9-71).

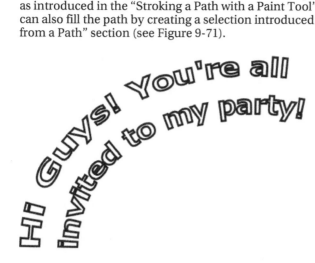

Figure 9-70. The path stroked with the Stroke Path dialog and a line width of three pixels

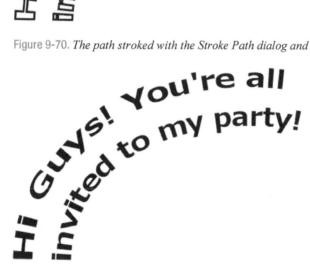

Figure 9-71. A selection was created out of the path and filled with a black foreground color.

Summary

This chapter used the toolbox and toolbox options to show you how to draw perfectly straight lines, circles, ellipses and squares. Also how to be creative and change these shapes and how to fill areas with color. You are introduced to the world of drawing tiny pictures in our pixel art section. There is a digital freehand section using the Paths Tool. Finally we show you how to create curving text.

CHAPTER 10

■ ■ ■

Hints, Tips, and Further Help

This chapter looks at some of the ways you can customize GIMP. We also show you where to find and add extra options such as plug-ins and extensions. We look at the similarities and differences between GIMP and Photoshop. There is a Troubleshooting section and information on where to go for further help.

Customizing GIMP

The Preferences dialog allows you to customize GIMP. You can ignore this area altogether or you can customize GIMP so that each time it opens, certain areas are arranged the way that you prefer. The Preferences dialog is available at Edit ➤ Preferences (see Figure 10-1).

There is a large range of options to customize. Here are are some that you might find useful:

- To change the size of a new blank image, go to Edit ➤ Preferences ➤ Default Image (see Figure 10-1).

- To change the spacing of the grid placed over an image when aligning items, go to Edit ➤ Preferences ➤ Default Grid.

- To change or turn off some of the items seen when you open your workspace, go to Edit ➤ Preferences ➤ Image Windows ➤ Appearance.

Most changes made in the Preferences dialog will not take effect until you restart GIMP. If you do not like the changes that you made in the Preferences area, you can always return to the default values by going back to the settings area and clicking Reset.

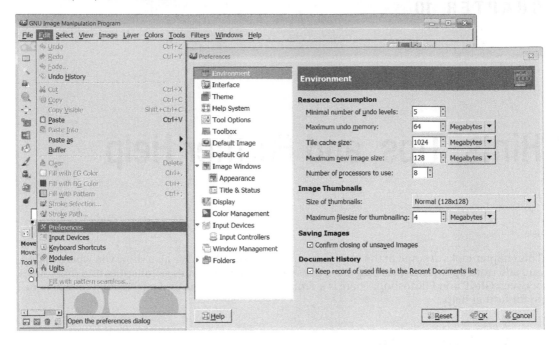

Figure 10-1. *GIMP's Preferences menu*

Increasing GIMP's Undo History

When GIMP is first loaded, there are only five undo steps. For example, if you make six brush strokes, you can only go back five steps in the Undo History. It is possible, however, to increase the number of steps in Undo History, as follows:

1. Go to Edit ➤ Preferences ➤ Environment (see Figure 10-1).

2. Under "Resource Consumption" go to "Minimal number of undo levels." Change this number to 20 or more.

3. Also, increase the "Maximum undo memory" to 200 or more.

4. Restart GIMP to make these changes take effect.

You can change these values at any time. To undo changes, hit the Reset button at the bottom of the Edit ➤ Preferences ➤ Environment page.

Scanning Images

Importing images from a scanner or camera is different on every operating system. For scanning, the application GIMP uses is based on your computer's operating system, as shown in Table 10-1.

Table 10-1.*Scanning with GIMP*

Operating System	Program	Access
Windows	Install the scanner driver. The driver will most likely support the TWAIN interface, which GIMP uses to communicate with the scanner.	File ➤ Create ➤ Scanner/Camera
Mac OS X	Install the scanner driver.	Applications/Scanner_Name
GNU/Linux (Ubuntu, Red Hat, SuSE)	Install the program XSane. (First, check the XSane homepage [www.xsane.org] to see if your scanner is supported.)	File ➤ Create ➤ XSane

With your scanner plugged into your computer, simply follow the scanner dialog. Once the scanner dialog imports the scanned image, it is sent to GIMP (see Figure 10-2). You can then edit the image in GIMP. The scanner dialog can be found at File ➤ Create ➤ Scanner.

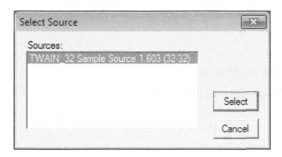

Figure 10-2. *The Windows source dialog to select your scanner*

GIMP Can Be Extended

It is possible to extend GIMP's functionality with Plug-ins and Extensions.

What is a Plug-in?

Plug-ins are extra brushes, patterns, color tables, 3D effects, filters, and more. GIMP has a large range of downloadable plug-ins. These extensions increase the functionality of GIMP. There are two types of plug-ins:

- Plug-ins that use the Python programming language and end with ".py" can be used on any operating system.

- Plug-ins with an ".exe" file extension are for Microsoft Windows only.

The central repository for downloading plug-ins is at http://registry.GIMP.org.

■ **Note** Plug-ins are not part of the core of GIMP. Some plug-ins are thoroughly tested and some are not. Check how popular a plug-in is and how old it is before you install it. You could try researching the plug-in name on Google for comments or reviews.

Installing Plug-ins

All new extensions or plug-ins go into one of the sub-folders in your GIMP user folder. The location of this folder depends on your version of GIMP and your operating system. The user folder keeps all your data, including patterns, saved tool settings, palettes, and plug-ins.

Windows

To install a Windows plug-in, do the following:

1. Download the plug-in.

2. Click the Windows Start symbol and click on your username.

3. In your username folder, open the GIMP folder (see Figure 10-3).

4. Copy the plug-in into the plug-in folder.

5. Restart GIMP.

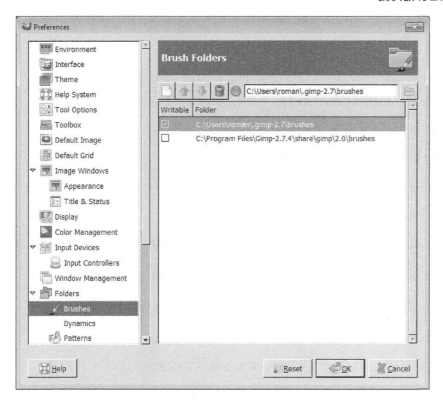

Figure 10-3. *An example of a user folder*

Mac OS X

To install a Mac OS X plug-in, do the following:

1. Download the plug-in.

2. Go to Users ➤ YourUserName ➤ Library ➤ Applications Support ➤ GIMP.

3. Open the GIMP folder and put the plug-in in the Plug-in folder.

4. Restart GIMP.

Ubuntu/Linux

To install an Ubuntu/Linux plug-in, do the following:

1. Download the plug-in.

2. Go to Places ➤ Home Folder.

3. Check the Show Hidden Files option, which is under View in the main menu.

4. Open your user folder, find the GIMP folder and open it.

5. Put the plug-in in the plug-in folder. (This is inside the GIMP folder.)

6. Restart GIMP.

You can check that your plug-in was installed by clicking Help in the top menu. Click Plug-In Browser to see the plug-in list.

GIMP Extension List

Extensions are installed by dropping them into their designated folder and restarting GIMP. Table 10-2 gives an overview of each folder's purpose.

Table 10-2. *List of GIMP folders and their extensions.*

Folder	File Extension	Dialog
brushes	.gih, .vbr, and .abr	Windows ➤ Dockable Dialogs ➤ Fonts
curves	No extension	Colors ➤ Curves
dynamics	No extension	Windows ➤ Dockable Dialogs ➤ Paint Dynamics
fonts	.ttf, .otf	Windows ➤ Dockable Dialogs ➤ Fonts
fractalexplorer	No extension	Filters ➤ Render ➤ Fractal Explorer
gfig	.fig or no extension	Filters ➤ Render ➤ Gfig
GIMPressionist	No extension	Filters ➤ Artistic ➤ GIMPressionist
gradients	.ggr	Windows ➤ Dockable Dialogs ➤ Gradients
levels	No extension	Colors ➤ Levels
palettes	.gpl, .ase	Windows ➤ Dockable Dialogs ➤ Palettes
patterns	.pat, .png	Windows ➤ Dockable Dialogs ➤ Patterns
modules	No extension. Executables like plug-ins	Edit ➤ Modules
plug-ins	.py, .dll, and .dylib	Register their own dialog
scripts	.scm	All scripts can be accessed under File ➤ Create
templates	No extension	New templates used in the New Image dialog under File ➤ New
themes	No extension	Can be used to customize all icons in GIMP. Managed under Edit ➤ Preferences ➤ Themes

Folder	File Extension	Dialog
tmp	No extension	For GIMP internal use only
tool presets	.gtp	Used to reload saved general tool settings used by all tools

Photoshop and GIMP: A Comparison

If you are a Photoshop user, please do not open GIMP and expect it to look and feel like Photoshop. GIMP does not try to mimic Photoshop's layout or behavior. If you have worked with Photoshop for some time you will find using GIMP more difficult to use than someone who has never used Photoshop. When you open GIMP for the first time, work on a simple task first and then slowly build on it.

GIMP	Photoshop
Cost – free	Cost – from US$1,299
Development - software built and shared globally by the GIMP community of volunteers (www.gimp.org).	Development – in house by Adobe (www.adobe.com).
License - GIMP is free to use and to copy the code under the GNU General Public License v3 (see Appendix B for the full license).	License - Photoshop has a restricted license; individuals and groups can buy the rights to use Photoshop but cannot reuse its code.
Platform - . GIMP is available for Windows, Mac, Linux, and most UNIX computers.	Platform - Photoshop is available for Windows and Mac computers.
HDR not supported	HDR supported

GIMP	Photoshop
Sharpening Filters are located in Filters ➤ Enhance.	Sharpening Filters are located in Filter ➤ Sharpen.
Adjustment layers – no	Adjustment layers – yes
16 bit handling – not yet	16 bit handling – yes
CMYK – not supported	CMYK – supported
Smart Objects – no	Smart Objects – yes

Continued

GIMP	Photoshop
User Interface – layers, selections and tools are in similar positions. Most other options are in different places	User Interface - layers, selections and tools are in similar positions. Most other options are in different places
User Interface - Single Window Mode option for Windows, Mac and Linux	User Interface - Single Window Mode for Windows
Non-blocking operations – GIMP will allow you to work on two or more images at once	Photoshop allows you to work on one image at a time only
Supports Layers	Supports Layers
PSD files open and save in GIMP with layers intact (but not adjustment layer information)	PSD files open with layers and adjustment layer information
Supports Masks	Supports Masks
Supports Selections	Supports Selections
Has a wide range of Filters	Has a wide range of Filters
Has Levels	Has Levels
Has Curves	Has Curves
Has a Toolbox	Has a Toolbox
Has an Undo History	Has an Undo History
Has a Text Tool	Has a Text Tool

GIMP and Photoshop on the Same Computer

In Windows it is possible to run GIMP and Photoshop on the same computer. You may get an error message when you add GIMP saying it needs a file, `Plug-ins.dll`. This occurs because Photoshop is using this file. Navigate to your Photoshop folder and copy the `Plug-ins.dll` file. Then, put the file into the System 32 folder of your Windows installation. Ask a friend to help if you are not sure where this is.

Troubleshooting GIMP

GIMP is a lot of fun, but occasionally new users can get confused. Here are some tips.

I Just Want One Workspace

You need to be in single-window mode. This option has been available since GIMP 2.8. In the top menu area, go to Windows ➤ Single Window Mode. The three windows are joined into one workspace. For further details, see Chapter 2.

I Cannot Seem to Paint or Fill My Image with a Color

This is most likely due to a wrong active layer or a small selection. To resolve, try following these pointers:

- From the Selection menu, deselect everything by going Select ➤ None. If you created a very tiny selection by accident, your paint tools will only fill this small selection. By deselecting everything, you can start over by painting or filling.

- A wrong layer is selected. Select the background layer in your layer dialog. The layer dialog is made visible by selecting Windows ➤ Dockable Dialogs ➤ Layers.

- Check that the image is not set to indexed mode by selecting Image ➤ Mode ➤ Indexed. If it is selected, then you can only paint with a small range of colors. This is caused by loading indexed images in the .gif format.

The Paint Tools Are Not Working

Check your layer dialog. Do you have an active floating selection in there (see Figure 10-4)?

Figure 10-4. *A floating selection can cause paint tools not to paint anymore.*

The floating selection becomes the active selection after you paste a copied image element. This takes precedence over all functionality because you may apply a filter or paint tool to the wrong layer.

Solve this by anchoring the selection, go to Layer ➤ Anchor Layer.

GIMP Will Not Let Me Do Anything

You may be working in GIMP and suddenly find you are prevented from doing anything. The most likely reason is that you have a dialog box or small window hiding underneath GIMP or underneath something else open on your desktop. Find the open dialog box and Click OK or cancel the dialog to continue working.

The other possibility is that you are editing large image files and are using too much RAM. Increasing GIMP's speed is covered later in this chapter.

Lost Toolbox or Other Dialogs

You lost your toolbox and all that you can see is an image window. To bring back your toolbox, do the following:

- Press CTRL+B for Windows or COMMAND+B for Mac or

- Click on Windows ➤ New Toolbox

If you cannot see important dialogs like layers and tool options, restore them by:

- Selecting Windows ➤ Recently Closed Docks, or

- Going to the sub-menu items under Windows ➤ Dockable Dialogs

Where Is Undo History?

If you have lost your Undo History in single-window mode, go to View ➤ Shrink Wrap. You should now see your Undo History on the right of your screen.

Resizing Your Workspace

To resize the GIMP workspace to the image size, use the View ➤ Shrink Wrap menu option.

Layer Control

If you are working with many layers, selecting layers can be a nuisance with the default setting of the move tool. Go to Edit ➤ Preferences and choose the Tool Options entry. Check the item labeled with "Set layer or path as active" under the Move tool option. Whenever you select an item in your image, it selects the corresponding layer.

How Do I Make Changes Outside a Selected Area?

Sometimes you need to select part of an image to isolate it from the changes you wish to make in adjacent areas. To make changes outside a selected area, go to Select ➤ Invert; the area outside your selection is activated. Any changes made will not affect the selected area.

How Do I Reset a Tool or Dialog?

GIMP allows you to reset every changed value back to the default. Every dialog has a Reset button next to the OK button. Click on the Reset button if you want to revert the current dialog values to default.

Improving GIMP's Speed

If you are waiting a long time for something to render in GIMP, it might be because you do not have enough memory (RAM) allocated. The best way to improve GIMP's speed is to allocate more memory to GIMP.

To change the amount of RAM, do the following:

1. Go to Edit ➤ Preferences. (Refer to Figure 10-1).

2. Click Environment. Under "Resource Consumption" set the Tile cache size to about half the memory on your computer. If you don't know how to find how much RAM you have on your computer, ask a friend to help you.

How Do I Get Maximum Editing Control of an Image?

Most images in GIMP use three channels by default: red, green, and blue. Exceptions are grayscale images or indexed images, which use a small number of colors. Therefore, just about every color photo you load into GIMP has three channels. You can see, select, and manage the channels in the channel dialog found under Windows ➤ Dockable Dialogs ➤ Channels (see Figure 10-5).

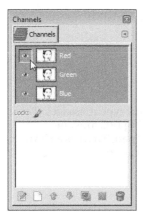

Figure 10-5. *The Channels dialog*

How do I Copy and Paste in GIMP

In Windows click Control C to copy and Control V to paste a selection. For Mac click Command C to copy and Command V to paste a selection. This new selection becomes a floating layer. You need to anchor the selection by going to Layer ➤ Anchor Layer.

How do I remove the Marching Ant Border around my Image

Go to View ➤ Show Layer Boundary to remove the border.

How do I open Raw Files

The up-to-date version of GIMP cannot open raw images on its own. If you want to edit raw images, you will need to install a plug-in called UFRaw. UFRaw converts your raw files so that they can be imported into GIMP. UFRaw is third-party software; however, some builds of GIMP for Mac are shipped with UFRaw preinstalled.

Further Help

Assistance is available from the Help menu in GIMP. However, if you click Help in GIMP, you may see the following message: "The GIMP user manual is not installed on your computer." Click the Read Online button or install the help package that is available for your operating system. Windows users should go to www.gimp.org/windows. Click the Installer. Under GIMP Help 2 there is a selection of Help documents available in more than a dozen languages. Select a language, then follow the prompts to install Help.

Additional help is available at www.gimp.org/links. This web page contains lists of tutorials, clubs, and communities. The large community of GIMP users and enthusiasts organize in forums, chat environments, and mailing lists.

Mailing Lists

GIMP has a number of mailing lists. There is a mailing list for people who use GIMP, as well as lists for the developers. An overview of all GIMP mailing lists are at www.GIMP.org/mail_lists.html.

IRC: Joining the GIMP Community

IRC stands for Internet Relay Chat. People on IRC do not actually talk—they type messages. These messages are seen by anyone logged in to a particular session. (People using IRC must be respectful or they may be removed.) IRC is one of the ways GIMP is developed. There is a GIMP channel for developers and another one for users. For further information go to www.gimp.org/irc.html.

Further Reading

The following books also cover GIMP:

- *GIMP 2.6 for Photographers* by Klaus Goelker (Rocky Nook, 2011)
- *GIMP Bible (2.6)* by Jason van Gumster and Robert Shimonski (Wiley, 2010)
- *Beginning GIMP: From Novice to Professional* by Akkana Peck (Apress, 2008)

Other Open-Source Graphics Software

GIMP is not the only free, open-source software program available for digital graphics. Depending on the task you want to solve, you might find another program more useful.

Inkscape

Inkscape's focus is on paths, not pixels (see Figure 10-6). Inkscape is a vector graphics editor that has similarities to CorelDRAW and Adobe Illustrator. You can export/import Inkscape illustrations into GIMP. Inkscape is often used to create illustrations or web site layouts. Inkscape is available for Windows, Mac, and Linux operating systems at http://inkscape.org.

Figure 10-6. *Inkscape can be used for creating illustrations based on paths.*

Scribus

Scribus is a desktop publishing program. It is suitable to create flyers, newspapers, and books. It uses advanced color-management systems and versatile PDF creation. Scribus has press-ready output and a fresh approach to page design. It is available for Windows, Mac, and Linux operating systems at www.scribus.net.

Blender

If you enjoy creating 3D images, Blender is an open-source, 3D content creation suite. Use it to create 3D characters and 3D animation. Blender is available for Windows, Mac, and Linux operating systems at www.blender.org.

GIMP's Future

GIMP (www.gimp.org) is under continual improvement by developers collaborating from various parts of the world.

APPENDIX A

Keyboard Shortcuts

Help

Commands		Result
	F1	Help
Shift +	F1	Context Help

Tools

Commands		Result
	R	Rect Select
	E	Ellipse Select
	F	Free Select
	Z	Fuzzy Select
Shift +	O	Select By Color
	I	Scissors
	B	Paths
	O	Color Picker
	M	Move

Continued

Commands		Result
Shift +	C	Crop and Resize
Shift +	R	Rotate
Shift +	T	Scale
Shift +	S	Shear
Shift +	P	Perspective
Shift +	F	Flip
	T	Text
Shift +	B	Bucket Fill
	L	Blend
	N	Pencil
	P	Paintbrush
Shift +	E	Eraser
	A	Airbrush
	K	Ink
	C	Clone
Shift +	U	Blur/Sharpen
	S	Smudge
Shift +	D	Dodge/Burn

Context

Commands				Result
			X	Swap Colors
			D	Default Colors
	Ctrl +		N	New image
	Ctrl +		O	Open image
	Ctrl +	Alt +	O	Open image as new layer
	Ctrl +		D	Duplicate image
	Ctrl +		1	Open recent image 01
	Ctrl +		2	Open recent image 02
	Ctrl +		3	Open recent image 03
	Ctrl +		4	Open recent image 04
	Ctrl +		5	Open recent image 05
	Ctrl +		6	Open recent image 06
	Ctrl +		7	Open recent image 07
	Ctrl +		8	Open recent image 08
	Ctrl +		9	Open recent image 09
	Ctrl +		0	Open recent image 10
	Ctrl +		S	Save image
Shift +	Ctrl +		S	Save under a new name
	Ctrl +		E	Export to
Shift +	Ctrl +		E	Export ...
	Ctrl +		Q	Quit
	Ctrl +		L	Layers

Continued

Commands			Result
Shift +	Ctrl +	B	Brushes
Shift +	Ctrl +	P	Patterns
	Ctrl +	G	Gradients
Shift +	Ctrl +	T	Tool Options
	Ctrl +	P	Palettes
Shift +	Ctrl +	I	Info window
Shift +	Ctrl +	N	Navigation window

Within a Dialog

Commands			Result
	Alt +	F4	
	Ctrl +	W	Close the window
		Tab	Jump to next widget
Shift +		Tab	Jump to previous widget
		Enter	Set the new value
		Space	
		Enter	Activate current button or list
	Ctrl +	Alt +	PgUp
	Ctrl +	PgDn	In a multi-tab dialog, switch tabs

Within a File Dialog

Commands			Result
Shift +		L	Open Location
	Alt +	Up arrow	Up-Folder
	Alt +	Down arrow	Down-Folder
	Alt +	Home	Home-Folder
		Esc	Close Dialog

Window

Commands			Result
		F10	Main Menu
Shift +		F10	
		right click	Drop-down Menu
		F11	Toggle fullscreen
Shift +		Q	Toggle quickmask
	Ctrl +	W	Close document window

Zoom

Commands			Result
		+	Zoom in
		-	Zoom out
		1	Zoom 1:1
	Ctrl +	E	Shrink wrap
Shift +	Ctrl +	E	Fit image in window
Shift +		mouse wheel	Zoom

Scrolling (Panning)

Commands			Result
Shift +		arrows	Scroll canvas
	Ctrl +	arrows	Jump to canvas borders
		middle button drag	Scroll canvas
		mouse wheel	Scroll canvas vertically
Shift +		mouse wheel	Scroll canvas horizontally

Rulers and Guides

Commands			Result
		mouse drag	Drag off a ruler to create guide
	Ctrl +	mouse drag	Drag a sample point out of the rulers
Shift +	Ctrl +	R	Toggle rulers
Shift +	Ctrl +	T	Toggle guides

Undo/Redo

Commands		Result
Ctrl +	Z	Undo
Ctrl +	Y	Redo

Clipboard

Commands			Result
	Ctrl +	C	Copy selection
	Ctrl +	X	Cut selection
	Ctrl +	V	Paste clipboard
	Ctrl +	K	Clears selection
Shift +	Ctrl +	C	Named copy selection
Shift +	Ctrl +	X	Named cut selection
Shift +	Ctrl +	V	Named paste clipboard

Fill

Commands			Result
			Erase selection
	Ctrl +	D	Fill with FG Color
	Ctrl +	D	Fill with BG Color
	Ctrl +	D	Fill with Pattern
		PgUp	
	Ctrl +	Tab	Select the layer above
		PgDn	
Shift +	Ctrl +	Tab	Select the layer below
		Home	Select the first layer
		End	Select the last layer
	Ctrl +	M	Merge visible layers
	Ctrl +	H	Anchor layer

Continued

Commands			Result
	Ctrl +	T	Toggle selections
	Ctrl +	A	Select all
Shift +	Ctrl +	A	Select none
	Ctrl +	I	Invert selection
Shift +	Ctrl +	L	Float selection
Shift +		V	Path to selection
	Ctrl +	F	Repeat last filter
Shift +	Ctrl +	F	Reshow last filter
Shift +		mouse click	Zoom in
Ctrl +		mouse click	Zoom out
		mouse drag	Zoom into the area

APPENDIX B

■ ■ ■

GNU General Public License

Preamble

The GNU General Public License is a free, copyleft license for software and other kinds of works.

The licenses for most software and other practical works are designed to take away your freedom to share and change the works. By contrast, the GNU General Public License is intended to guarantee your freedom to share and change all versions of a program—to make sure it remains free software for all its users. We, the Free Software Foundation, use the GNU General Public License for most of our software; it applies also to any other work released this way by its authors. You can apply it to your programs, too.

When we speak of free software, we are referring to freedom, not price. Our General Public Licenses are designed to make sure that you have the freedom to distribute copies of free software (and charge for them if you wish), that you receive source code or can get it if you want it, that you can change the software or use pieces of it in new free programs, and that you know you can do these things.

To protect your rights, we need to prevent others from denying you these rights or asking you to surrender the rights. Therefore, you have certain responsibilities if you distribute copies of the software, or if you modify it: responsibilities to respect the freedom of others.

For example, if you distribute copies of such a program, whether gratis or for a fee, you must pass on to the recipients the same freedoms that you received. You must make sure that they, too, receive or can get the source code. And you must show them these terms so they know their rights.

Developers that use the GNU GPL protect your rights with two steps: (1) assert copyright on the software, and (2) offer you this License giving you legal permission to copy, distribute and/or modify it.

For the developers' and authors' protection, the GPL clearly explains that there is no warranty for this free software. For both users' and authors' sake, the GPL requires that modified versions be marked as changed, so that their problems will not be attributed erroneously to authors of previous versions.

Some devices are designed to deny users access to install or run modified versions of the software inside them, although the manufacturer can do so. This is fundamentally incompatible with the aim of protecting users' freedom to change the software. The systematic pattern of such abuse occurs in the area of products for individuals to use, which is precisely where it is most unacceptable. Therefore, we have designed this version of the GPL to prohibit the practice for those products. If such problems arise substantially in other domains, we stand ready to extend this provision to those domains in future versions of the GPL, as needed to protect the freedom of users.

Finally, every program is threatened constantly by software patents. States should not allow patents to restrict development and use of software on general-purpose computers, but in those that do, we wish to avoid the special danger that patents applied to a free program could make it effectively proprietary. To prevent this, the GPL assures that patents cannot be used to render the program non-free.

The precise terms and conditions for copying, distribution and modification follow.

Terms and Conditions

0. Definitions

"This License" refers to version 3 of the GNU General Public License.

"Copyright" also means copyright-like laws that apply to other kinds of works, such as semiconductor masks.

"The Program" refers to any copyrightable work licensed under this License. Each licensee is addressed as "you". "Licensees" and "recipients" may be individuals or organizations.

To "modify" a work means to copy from or adapt all or part of the work in a fashion requiring copyright permission, other than the making of an exact copy. The resulting work is called a "modified version" of the earlier work or a work "based on" the earlier work.

A "covered work" means either the unmodified Program or a work based on the Program.

To "propagate" a work means to do anything with it that, without permission, would make you directly or secondarily liable for infringement under applicable copyright law, except executing it on a computer or modifying a private copy. Propagation includes copying, distribution (with or without modification), making available to the public, and in some countries other activities as well.

To "convey" a work means any kind of propagation that enables other parties to make or receive copies. Mere interaction with a user through a computer network, with no transfer of a copy, is not conveying.

An interactive user interface displays "Appropriate Legal Notices" to the extent that it includes a convenient and prominently visible feature that (1) displays an appropriate copyright notice, and (2) tells the user that there is no warranty for the work (except to the extent that warranties are provided), that licensees may convey the work under this License, and how to view a copy of this License. If the interface presents a list of user commands or options, such as a menu, a prominent item in the list meets this criterion.

1. Source Code

The "source code" for a work means the preferred form of the work for making modifications to it. "Object code" means any non-source form of a work.

A "Standard Interface" means an interface that either is an official standard defined by a recognized standards body, or, in the case of interfaces specified for a particular programming language, one that is widely used among developers working in that language.

The "System Libraries" of an executable work include anything, other than the work as a whole, that (a) is included in the normal form of packaging a Major Component, but which is not part of that Major Component, and (b) serves only to enable use of the work with that Major Component, or to implement a Standard Interface for which an implementation is available to the public in source code form. A "Major Component", in this context, means a major essential component (kernel, window system, and so on) of the specific operating system (if any) on which the executable work runs, or a compiler used to produce the work, or an object code interpreter used to run it.

The "Corresponding Source" for a work in object code form means all the source code needed to generate, install, and (for an executable work) run the object code and to modify the work, including scripts to control those activities. However, it does not include the work's System Libraries, or general-purpose tools or generally available free programs which are used unmodified in performing those activities but which are not part of the work. For example, Corresponding Source includes interface definition files associated with source files for the work, and the source code for shared libraries and dynamically linked subprograms that the work is specifically designed to require, such as by intimate data communication or control flow between those subprograms and other parts of the work.

The Corresponding Source need not include anything that users can regenerate automatically from other parts of the Corresponding Source.

The Corresponding Source for a work in source code form is that same work.

2. Basic Permissions

All rights granted under this License are granted for the term of copyright on the Program, and are irrevocable provided the stated conditions are met. This License explicitly affirms your unlimited permission to run the unmodified Program. The output from running a covered work is covered by this License only if the output, given its content, constitutes a covered work. This License acknowledges your rights of fair use or other equivalent, as provided by copyright law.

You may make, run and propagate covered works that you do not convey, without conditions so long as your license otherwise remains in force. You may convey covered works to others for the sole purpose of having them make modifications exclusively for you, or provide you with facilities for running those works, provided that you comply with the terms of this License in conveying all material for which you do not control copyright. Those thus making or running the covered works for you must do so exclusively on your behalf, under your direction and control, on terms that prohibit them from making any copies of your copyrighted material outside their relationship with you.

Conveying under any other circumstances is permitted solely under the conditions stated below. Sublicensing is not allowed; section 10 makes it unnecessary.

3. Protecting Users' Legal Rights from Anti-Circumvention Law

No covered work shall be deemed part of an effective technological measure under any applicable law fulfilling obligations under article 11 of the WIPO copyright treaty adopted on 20 December 1996, or similar laws prohibiting or restricting circumvention of such measures.

When you convey a covered work, you waive any legal power to forbid circumvention of technological measures to the extent such circumvention is effected by exercising rights under this License with respect to the covered work, and you disclaim any intention to limit operation or modification of the work as a means of enforcing, against the work's users, your or third parties' legal rights to forbid circumvention of technological measures.

4. Conveying Verbatim Copies

You may convey verbatim copies of the Program's source code as you receive it, in any medium, provided that you conspicuously and appropriately publish on each copy an appropriate copyright notice; keep intact all notices stating that this License and any non-permissive terms added in accord with section 7 apply to the code; keep intact all notices of the absence of any warranty; and give all recipients a copy of this License along with the Program.

You may charge any price or no price for each copy that you convey, and you may offer support or warranty protection for a fee.

5. Conveying Modified Source Versions

You may convey a work based on the Program, or the modifications to produce it from the Program, in the form of source code under the terms of section 4, provided that you also meet all of these conditions:

a) The work must carry prominent notices stating that you modified it, and giving a relevant date.

b) The work must carry prominent notices stating that it is released under this License and any conditions added under section 7. This requirement modifies the requirement in section 4 to "keep intact all notices".

c) You must license the entire work, as a whole, under this License to anyone who comes into possession of a copy. This License will therefore apply, along with any applicable section 7 additional terms, to the whole of the work, and all its parts, regardless of how they are packaged. This License gives no permission to license the work in any other way, but it does not invalidate such permission if you have separately received it.

d) If the work has interactive user interfaces, each must display Appropriate Legal Notices; however, if the Program has interactive interfaces that do not display Appropriate Legal Notices, your work need not make them do so.

A compilation of a covered work with other separate and independent works, which are not by their nature extensions of the covered work, and which are not combined with it such as to form a larger program, in or on a volume of a storage or distribution medium, is called an "aggregate" if the compilation and its resulting copyright are not used to limit the access or legal rights of the compilation's users beyond what the individual works permit. Inclusion of a covered work in an aggregate does not cause this License to apply to the other parts of the aggregate.

6. Conveying Non-Source Forms

You may convey a covered work in object code form under the terms of sections 4 and 5, provided that you also convey the machine-readable Corresponding Source under the terms of this License, in one of these ways:

a) Convey the object code in, or embodied in, a physical product (including a physical distribution medium), accompanied by the Corresponding Source fixed on a durable physical medium customarily used for software interchange.

b) Convey the object code in, or embodied in, a physical product (including a physical distribution medium), accompanied by a written offer, valid for at least three years and valid for as long as you offer spare parts or customer support for that product model, to give anyone who possesses the object code either (1) a copy of the Corresponding Source for all the software in the product that is covered by this License, on a durable physical medium customarily used for software interchange, for a price no more than your reasonable cost of physically performing this conveying of source, or (2) access to copy the Corresponding Source from a network server at no charge.

c) Convey individual copies of the object code with a copy of the written offer to provide the Corresponding Source. This alternative is allowed only occasionally and noncommercially, and only if you received the object code with such an offer, in accord with subsection 6b.

d) Convey the object code by offering access from a designated place (gratis or for a charge), and offer equivalent access to the Corresponding Source in the same way through the same place at no further charge. You need not require recipients to copy the Corresponding Source along with the object code. If the place to copy the object code is a network server, the Corresponding Source may be on a different server (operated by you or a third party) that supports equivalent copying facilities, provided you maintain clear directions next to the object code saying where to find the Corresponding Source. Regardless of what server hosts the Corresponding Source, you remain obligated to ensure that it is available for as long as needed to satisfy these requirements.

e) Convey the object code using peer-to-peer transmission, provided you inform other peers where the object code and Corresponding Source of the work are being offered to the general public at no charge under subsection 6d.

A separable portion of the object code, whose source code is excluded from the Corresponding Source as a System Library, need not be included in conveying the object code work.

A "User Product" is either (1) a "consumer product", which means any tangible personal property which is normally used for personal, family, or household purposes, or (2) anything designed or sold for incorporation into a dwelling. In determining whether a product is a consumer product, doubtful cases shall be resolved in favor of coverage. For a particular product received by a particular user, "normally used" refers to a typical or common use of that class of product, regardless of the status of the particular user or of the way in which the particular user actually uses, or expects or is expected to use, the product. A product is a consumer product regardless of whether the product has substantial commercial, industrial or non-consumer uses, unless such uses represent the only significant mode of use of the product.

"Installation Information" for a User Product means any methods, procedures, authorization keys, or other information required to install and execute modified versions of a covered work in that User Product from a modified version of its Corresponding Source. The information must suffice to ensure that the continued functioning of the modified object code is in no case prevented or interfered with solely because modification has been made.

If you convey an object code work under this section in, or with, or specifically for use in, a User Product, and the conveying occurs as part of a transaction in which the right of possession and use of the User Product is transferred to the recipient in perpetuity or for a fixed term (regardless of how the transaction is characterized), the Corresponding Source conveyed under this section must be accompanied by the Installation Information. But this requirement does not apply if neither you nor any third party retains the ability to install modified object code on the User Product (for example, the work has been installed in ROM).

The requirement to provide Installation Information does not include a requirement to continue to provide support service, warranty, or updates for a work that has been modified or installed by the recipient, or for the User Product in which it has been modified or installed. Access to a network may be denied when the modification itself materially and adversely affects the operation of the network or violates the rules and protocols for communication across the network.

Corresponding Source conveyed, and Installation Information provided, in accord with this section must be in a format that is publicly documented (and with an implementation available to the public in source code form), and must require no special password or key for unpacking, reading or copying.

7. Additional Terms

"Additional permissions" are terms that supplement the terms of this License by making exceptions from one or more of its conditions.

Additional permissions that are applicable to the entire Program shall be treated as though they were included in this License, to the extent that they are valid under applicable law. If additional permissions apply only to part of the Program, that part may be used separately under those permissions, but the entire Program remains governed by this License without regard to the additional permissions.

When you convey a copy of a covered work, you may at your option remove any additional permissions from that copy, or from any part of it. (Additional permissions may be written to require their own removal in certain cases when you modify the work.)You may place additional permissions on material, added by you to a covered work, for which you have or can give appropriate copyright permission.

Notwithstanding any other provision of this License, for material you add to a covered work, you may (if authorized by the copyright holders of that material) supplement the terms of this License with terms:

a) Disclaiming warranty or limiting liability differently from the terms of sections 15 and 16 of this License; or

b) Requiring preservation of specified reasonable legal notices or author attributions in that material or in the Appropriate Legal Notices displayed by works containing it; or

c) Prohibiting misrepresentation of the origin of that material, or requiring that modified versions of such material be marked in reasonable ways as different from the original version; or

d)   Limiting the use for publicity purposes of names of licensors or authors of the material; or

e)   Declining to grant rights under trademark law for use of some trade names, trademarks, or service marks; or

f)   Requiring indemnification of licensors and authors of that material by anyone who conveys the material (or modified versions of it) with contractual assumptions of liability to the recipient, for any liability that these contractual assumptions directly impose on those licensors and authors.

All other non-permissive additional terms are considered "further restrictions" within the meaning of section 10. If the Program as you received it, or any part of it, contains a notice stating that it is governed by this License along with a term that is a further restriction, you may remove that term. If a license document contains a further restriction but permits relicensing or conveying under this License, you may add to a covered work material governed by the terms of that license document, provided that the further restriction does not survive such relicensing or conveying.

If you add terms to a covered work in accord with this section, you must place, in the relevant source files, a statement of the additional terms that apply to those files, or a notice indicating where to find the applicable terms.

Additional terms, permissive or non-permissive, may be stated in the form of a separately written license, or stated as exceptions; the above requirements apply either way.

8. Termination

You may not propagate or modify a covered work except as expressly provided under this License. Any attempt otherwise to propagate or modify it is void, and will automatically terminate your rights under this License (including any patent licenses granted under the third paragraph of section 11).

However, if you cease all violation of this License, then your license from a particular copyright holder is reinstated (a) provisionally, unless and until the copyright holder explicitly and finally terminates your license, and (b) permanently, if the copyright holder fails to notify you of the violation by some reasonable means prior to 60 days after the cessation.

Moreover, your license from a particular copyright holder is reinstated permanently if the copyright holder notifies you of the violation by some reasonable means, this is the first time you have received notice of violation of this License (for any work) from that copyright holder, and you cure the violation prior to 30 days after your receipt of the notice.

Termination of your rights under this section does not terminate the licenses of parties who have received copies or rights from you under this License. If your rights have been terminated and not permanently reinstated, you do not qualify to receive new licenses for the same material under section 10.

9. Acceptance Not Required for Having Copies

You are not required to accept this License in order to receive or run a copy of the Program. Ancillary propagation of a covered work occurring solely as a consequence of using peer-to-peer transmission to receive a copy likewise does not require acceptance. However, nothing other than this License grants you permission to propagate or modify any covered work. These actions infringe copyright if you do not accept this License. Therefore, by modifying or propagating a covered work, you indicate your acceptance of this License to do so.

10. Automatic Licensing of Downstream Recipients

Each time you convey a covered work, the recipient automatically receives a license from the original licensors, to run, modify and propagate that work, subject to this License. You are not responsible for enforcing compliance by third parties with this License.

An "entity transaction" is a transaction transferring control of an organization, or substantially all assets of one, or subdividing an organization, or merging organizations. If propagation of a covered work results from an entity transaction, each party to that transaction who receives a copy of the work also receives whatever licenses to the work the party's predecessor in interest had or could give under the previous paragraph, plus a right to possession of the Corresponding Source of the work from the predecessor in interest, if the predecessor has it or can get it with reasonable efforts.

You may not impose any further restrictions on the exercise of the rights granted or affirmed under this License. For example, you may not impose a license fee, royalty, or other charge for exercise of rights granted under this License, and you may not initiate litigation (including a cross-claim or counterclaim in a lawsuit) alleging that any patent claim is infringed by making, using, selling, offering for sale, or importing the Program or any portion of it.

11. Patents

A "contributor" is a copyright holder who authorizes use under this License of the Program or a work on which the Program is based. The work thus licensed is called the contributor's "contributor version".

A contributor's "essential patent claims" are all patent claims owned or controlled by the contributor, whether already acquired or hereafter acquired, that would be infringed by some manner, permitted by this License, of making, using, or selling its contributor version, but do not include claims that would be infringed only as a consequence of further modification of the contributor version. For purposes of this definition, "control" includes the right to grant patent sublicenses in a manner consistent with the requirements of this License.

Each contributor grants you a non-exclusive, worldwide, royalty-free patent license under the contributor's essential patent claims, to make, use, sell, offer for sale, import and otherwise run, modify and propagate the contents of its contributor version.

In the following three paragraphs, a "patent license" is any express agreement or commitment, however denominated, not to enforce a patent (such as an express permission to practice a patent or covenant not to sue for patent infringement). To "grant" such a patent license to a party means to make such an agreement or commitment not to enforce a patent against the party.

If you convey a covered work, knowingly relying on a patent license, and the Corresponding Source of the work is not available for anyone to copy, free of charge and under the terms of this License, through a publicly available network server or other readily accessible means, then you must either (1) cause the Corresponding Source to be so available, or (2) arrange to deprive yourself of the benefit of the patent license for this particular work, or (3) arrange, in a manner consistent with the requirements of this License, to extend the patent license to downstream recipients. "Knowingly relying" means you have actual knowledge that, but for the patent license, your conveying the covered work in a country, or your recipient's use of the covered work in a country, would infringe one or more identifiable patents in that country that you have reason to believe are valid.

If, pursuant to or in connection with a single transaction or arrangement, you convey, or propagate by procuring conveyance of, a covered work, and grant a patent license to some of the parties receiving the covered work authorizing them to use, propagate, modify or convey a specific copy of the covered work, then the patent license you grant is automatically extended to all recipients of the covered work and works based on it.

A patent license is "discriminatory" if it does not include within the scope of its coverage, prohibits the exercise of, or is conditioned on the non-exercise of one or more of the rights that are specifically granted under this License. You may not convey a covered work if you are a party to an arrangement with a third party that is in the business of distributing software, under which you make payment to the third party based on the extent of your activity of conveying the work, and under which the third party grants, to any of the parties who would receive the covered work from you, a discriminatory patent license (a) in connection with copies of the covered work conveyed by you (or copies made from those copies), or (b) primarily for and in connection with specific products or compilations that contain the covered work, unless you entered into that arrangement, or that patent license was granted, prior to 28 March 2007.

Nothing in this License shall be construed as excluding or limiting any implied license or other defenses to infringement that may otherwise be available to you under applicable patent law.

12. No Surrender of Others' Freedom

If conditions are imposed on you (whether by court order, agreement or otherwise) that contradict the conditions of this License, they do not excuse you from the conditions of this License. If you cannot convey a covered work so as to satisfy simultaneously your obligations under this License and any other pertinent obligations, then as a consequence you may not convey it at all. For example, if you agree to terms that obligate you to collect a royalty for further conveying from those to whom you convey the Program, the only way you could satisfy both those terms and this License would be to refrain entirely from conveying the Program.

13. Use with the GNU Affero General Public License

Notwithstanding any other provision of this License, you have permission to link or combine any covered work with a work licensed under version 3 of the GNU Affero General Public License into a single combined work, and to convey the resulting work. The terms of this License will continue to apply to the part which is the covered work, but the special requirements of the GNU Affero General Public License, section 13, concerning interaction through a network will apply to the combination as such.

14. Revised Versions of this License

The Free Software Foundation may publish revised and/or new versions of the GNU General Public License from time to time. Such new versions will be similar in spirit to the present version, but may differ in detail to address new problems or concerns.

Each version is given a distinguishing version number. If the Program specifies that a certain numbered version of the GNU General Public License "or any later version" applies to it, you have the option of following the terms and conditions either of that numbered version or of any later version published by the Free Software Foundation. If the Program does not specify a version number of the GNU General Public License, you may choose any version ever published by the Free Software Foundation.

If the Program specifies that a proxy can decide which future versions of the GNU General Public License can be used, that proxy's public statement of acceptance of a version permanently authorizes you to choose that version for the Program.

Later license versions may give you additional or different permissions. However, no additional obligations are imposed on any author or copyright holder as a result of your choosing to follow a later version.

15. Disclaimer of Warranty

THERE IS NO WARRANTY FOR THE PROGRAM, TO THE EXTENT PERMITTED BY APPLICABLE LAW. EXCEPT WHEN OTHERWISE STATED IN WRITING THE COPYRIGHT HOLDERS AND/OR OTHER PARTIES PROVIDE THE PROGRAM "AS IS" WITHOUT WARRANTY OF ANY KIND, EITHER EXPRESSED OR IMPLIED, INCLUDING, BUT NOT LIMITED TO, THE IMPLIED WARRANTIES OF MERCHANTABILITY AND FITNESS FOR A PARTICULAR PURPOSE. THE ENTIRE RISK AS TO THE QUALITY AND PERFORMANCE OF THE PROGRAM IS WITH YOU. SHOULD THE PROGRAM PROVE DEFECTIVE, YOU ASSUME THE COST OF ALL NECESSARY SERVICING, REPAIR OR CORRECTION.

16. Limitation of Liability

IN NO EVENT UNLESS REQUIRED BY APPLICABLE LAW OR AGREED TO IN WRITING WILL ANY COPYRIGHT HOLDER, OR ANY OTHER PARTY WHO MODIFIES AND/OR CONVEYS THE PROGRAM AS PERMITTED ABOVE, BE LIABLE TO YOU FOR DAMAGES, INCLUDING ANY GENERAL, SPECIAL, INCIDENTAL OR CONSEQUENTIAL DAMAGES ARISING OUT OF THE USE OR INABILITY TO USE THE PROGRAM (INCLUDING BUT NOT LIMITED TO LOSS OF DATA OR DATA BEING RENDERED INACCURATE OR LOSSES SUSTAINED BY YOU OR THIRD PARTIES OR A FAILURE OF THE PROGRAM TO OPERATE WITH ANY OTHER PROGRAMS), EVEN IF SUCH HOLDER OR OTHER PARTY HAS BEEN ADVISED OF THE POSSIBILITY OF SUCH DAMAGES.

17. Interpretation of Sections 15 and 16

If the disclaimer of warranty and limitation of liability provided above cannot be given local legal effect according to their terms, reviewing courts shall apply local law that most closely approximates an absolute waiver of all civil liability in connection with the Program, unless a warranty or assumption of liability accompanies a copy of the Program in return for a fee.

END OF TERMS AND CONDITIONS

How to Apply These Terms to Your New Programs

If you develop a new program, and you want it to be of the greatest possible use to the public, the best way to achieve this is to make it free software which everyone can redistribute and change under these terms.

To do so, attach the following notices to the program. It is safest to attach them to the start of each source file to most effectively state the exclusion of warranty; and each file should have at least the "copyright" line and a pointer to where the full notice is found.

<one line to give the program's name and a brief idea of what it does. >
Copyright (C) <year><name of author>
This program is free software: you can redistribute it and/or modify it under the terms of the GNU General Public License as published by the Free Software Foundation, either version 3 of the License, or (at your option) any later version.

This program is distributed in the hope that it will be useful, but WITHOUT ANY WARRANTY; without even the implied warranty of MERCHANTABILITY or FITNESS FOR A PARTICULAR PURPOSE. See the GNU General Public License for more details.

You should have received a copy of the GNU General Public License along with this program. If not, see <http://www.gnu.org/licenses/>.

Also add information on how to contact you by electronic and paper mail.

If the program does terminal interaction, make it output a short notice like this when it starts in an interactive mode: <program>Copyright (C) <year><name of author>

This program comes with ABSOLUTELY NO WARRANTY; for details type `show w'.

This is free software, and you are welcome to redistribute it under certain conditions; type `show c' for details.

The hypothetical commands `show w' and `show c' should show the appropriate parts of the General Public License. Of course, your program's commands might be different; for a GUI interface, you would use an "about box".

You should also get your employer (if you work as a programmer) or school, if any, to sign a "copyright disclaimer" for the program, if necessary.

For more information on this, and how to apply and follow the GNU GPL, see <http://www.gnu.org/licenses/>.

The GNU General Public License does not permit incorporating your program into proprietary programs. If your program is a subroutine library, you may consider it more useful to permit linking proprietary applications with the library. If this is what you want to do, use the GNU Lesser General Public License instead of this License. But first, please read <http://www.gnu.org/philosophy/why-not-lgpl.html>.

Glossary

Alpha

A pixel has red, green, and blue values; a pixel also has an alpha value. The alpha value refers to the transparency value of the pixel. A 0 value means the pixel is transparent; at the other end of the scale, at 255, a pixel is fully opaque.

Not all file formats support transparency. PNG, PSD, TIF, and XCF all support transparency.

Alpha Channel

An alpha channel is used to represent the alpha value in an image.

Aspect Ratio

The aspect ratio of an image is the ratio between the width and height of an image. The first number refers to the width.

Brightness

Brightness refers to the amount of light in a color. If a red look unnaturally dark—it may need more brightness. If an aspect of the image lacks definition—it may have too much brightness. (See also Value. GIMP uses the term Value to denote the brightness or darkness of a color.)

Color Cast

A color cast is the term for a photo with an unnatural tinge or color across the entire photo. This happens when a photo is scanned, or with an old photo that has had its color quality degrade over time. Alternatively, the white balance in a digital camera may have been on the wrong setting. A safe setting for beginners is to set the white balance to automatic. Color Casts are repaired in GIMP using the Colors ➤ Levels option.

Convert to RGB Working Space

This message appears when you are opening an image with a color profile, such as Adobe RGB, attached. "Yes" will convert your image to RGB. This is the standard used by the internet, computer printers, and most printing shops.

Crop

To crop an image means to remove some of the edges of the original image. Cropping can be very useful to improve the artistic qualities of an image, particularly when you crop out something distracting.

Curves

Curves is a GIMP tool that works on the brightness, contrast, and midtones in an image. Like the Levels tool, you can work on the entire image or work on the red, blue, and green color channels separately. The curves tool offers more control than most other GIMP color options.

Dialog

A dialog is a small panel or window that contains options and settings for tool or menu items.

Dock

A dock is a dialog window, which can collect all dockable dialogs under Windows ➤ Dockable Dialogs.

Docking

Docking is moving individual docks around. You can detach a dock by dragging it. It can then stand alone or it can be docked elsewhere in the workspace.

Dot for Dot

With Dot for Dot activated, every pixel in the image is displayed as one pixel on the screen. This mode is useful for web images. However, if you are working on images to be printed, disable Dot for Dot. To disable Dot for Dot, go to View ➤ Dot for Dot and uncheck Dot for Dot. (Note that this only unchecks Dot for Dot for the current image. To deactivate Dot for Dot permanently, go to Edit ➤ Preferences ➤ Image Window and uncheck "Dot for Dot" by default and click OK.)

EXIF Data

Most digital cameras provide extra data about an image. This information is usually about the camera model and camera settings such as shutter setting, image date, image size, and file size. To view this image data in GIMP, go to File ➤ Properties ➤ Advanced Tab.

Export/Save Images

Apart from GIMP's native file format, XCF is saved using File ➤ Save; all other file formats use File ➤ Export.

GIMP

The acronym for GNU Image Manipulation Program. Originally called The GIMP, the digital image editing program's official name is now GIMP.

Guides

Single lines dragged from the ruler in GIMP's workspace. They can be helpful for positioning text and web site layouts.

Grid

Grids are useful to line up elements in an image. To access the grid, go to View ➤ Show Grid in the top menu. Also see Snap to Grid.

Help

Windows users can get assistance by selecting Help ➤ Online Help in the top menu. Help can also be accessible by pressing F1 on your keyboard.

HDR

HDR stands for High Dynamic Range. Three or more bracketed exposures of an image are sandwiched together to increase the dynamic range. GIMP supports this option via a plug-in called Exposure Blend.

Histogram

The Histogram gives a visual representation of the tonal and color information for the image. The default value setting displays the tonal and color information for the entire image. It is possible to change the value to red, blue, green, or alpha to view individual channel information for the image.

Hue

Hue is the aspect of the color that is yellow or red. If the skin tones or clouds in an image do not look natural, it is most likely because the hue is incorrect. If the photo looks very realistic, it is most likely because the image has the correct hue. Saturation, hue, and brightness make up the colors in an image.

Inkscape

Inkscape is an open-source editor for vector images.

Interactive Boundary

With the option enabled in some Selection Tools, the mouse can be used to adjust the edges of the completed selection.

Levels

Levels is a dialog available at Colors ➤ Levels. Beginners can select the Auto button for additional even tones in their image.

LZW

LZW (Lempie-Zif-Welch) is a lossless compression format. The compression process does not delete data. LZW is available in GIMP when exporting (saving) TIF files.

Pixel

A pixel is the smallest element in a digital image. GIMP edits pixels.

Pixel Art

Each pixel in a painting is individually painted. This gives a lot of clarity to an image. Early computer games used pixel art. This retro form of computer art still has a following because mobile phones and other digital devices have low resolution displays. Pixel art has a small file size and usually is saved as a PNG or GIF image. Favicons are often made from pixel art.

Plug-in

Plug-ins are extensions to GIMP's functionality. A plug-in is an external program that runs inside GIMP and interacts with GIMP. Some plug-ins have been thoroughly tested, while others have not. Plug-ins are located at `http://registry.gimp.org`.

Raster Images

GIMP edits raster images. A raster image uses a bitmap data structure to capture images.

Saturation

Saturation refers to the strength of color in an image. If the image looks washed out, then it is lacking saturation. If the image has too much color, it is oversaturated. Hue, saturation, and value (HSV) are the three aspects making up color in an image. GIMP uses RGB color by default and HSV directly relates to RGB color manipulations.

Save

XCF is the only file format saved from the Save menu within GIMP. All other file formats use the Export menu to save images.

Scaling

An image can be made smaller by scaling-down or larger by scaling-up an image. Also known as resizing.

Scale-Up

To scale-up an image means that an image's dimensions are made larger. This may mean a loss of image quality.

Sharpening

Unlike film photographs, a sharpening tool can improve most digital photographs. The digitizing process produces slightly out-of-focus images. The most useful tool in GIMP for sharpening photos is the Unsharp Mask found in Filters ➤ Enhance ➤ Unsharp Mask. There is also a tool called Sharpen. Sharpen highlights the edges in photos, but also the noise. Unsharp Mask gives a more natural result.

Snap to Grid

With this setting enabled, any object moved within eight pixels distance of the grid will snap to the grid. To activate Snap to Grid, go to View ➤ Snap to Grid in the top menu. To change the snapping distance, go to Edit ➤ Preferences ➤ Tool Options and change the "Snap distance." The snap distance is measured in pixels.

Snap to Guide

With this setting enabled, any object moved within eight pixels distance of the guide will snap to the guide. To activate Snap to Guide, go to View ➤ Snap to Guide in the top menu. To change the snapping distance, go to Edit ➤ Preferences ➤ Tool Options and change the "Snap distance." The snap distance is measured in pixels.

Tonal Range

The tonal range of an image refers to the brightest part through to the darkest part of an image. GIMP's Curves and Levels tools display the tonal range of an image in graph form.

Undo

To undo the last step, press Control+Z or go to Edit ➤ Undo in the menu. See also Undo History.

Undo History

GIMP does a limited number undo steps by default. To increase this number, go to Edit ➤ Preferences ➤ Environment.

Unsharp Mask

Use this tool for sharpening your images (rather than the less sophisticated Sharpen option). Unsharp Mask is found at Filters ➤ Enhance ➤ Unsharp Mask.

Value

Value simply refers to the brightness or darkness of a color. Hue, saturation, and value (HSV) work together to form color images. GIMP's digital editing uses RGB color by default.

Vector Images

Vector images use geometrical points, lines, and curves to represent an image.

XCF

XCF is GIMP's native file format. XCF stores all the raw data of an image file. If you intend to do extensive work on an image, save the image as an XCF file. XCF is only readable in GIMP. When you have finished working on an image, export the XCF file as a TIF, JPG, or other file format. XCF files contain information about layers, the pixel data for each layer, and the current selection; it records channels if there are any, as well as paths and guides. You can save your XCF image repeatedly with no loss of quality. In contrast, each time you save a JPG, some of the data is lost or modified.
One thing to note, XCF files do not record the Undo History.

Zoom

There are many ways to zoom in GIMP, as follows:

- Zoom using the following keyboard numbers:
    - 1 = 100%
    - 2 = 200%
    - 3 = 400%
    - 4 = 800%
    - 5 = 1600%
- Zoom via the menu options: View ➤ Zoom
- Zoom via the pull-down menu at the bottom edge of the workspace window
- Zoom using the Magnifying Tool in the Toolbox
- Keyboard shortcuts for zooming:
    - Fit image in window: Shift+Ctrl+E
    - Zoom In: +
    - Zoom Out: -

Index

U

V

CPSIA information can be obtained at www.ICGtesting.com
Printed in the USA
LVOW02s2230300614

392346LV00013B/791/P